The I in TEAM

Kristine—
good luck
teaming!
Susan

ACCELERATING PERFORMANCE OF
REMOTE AND CO-LOCATED TEAMS

The I in TEAM

SUSAN K. GERKE LINDA V. BERENS

UNITE
BUSINESS PRESS
A DIVISION OF TELOS PUBLICATIONS

Published By:
Unite Business Press, A division of Telos Publications
P.O. Box 4457, Huntington Beach, California 92605-4457
Toll Free 1-866-416-8973 / Phone 1-714-965-7696 / Fax 1-714-965-7697
http://www.telospublications.com

PRINTED IN THE UNITED STATES OF AMERICA

Cover/Layout Design/Illustrations: Visibility Designs

Library of Congress Cataloging-in-Publication Data

Gerke, Susan K.
  The I in team : accelerating performance of remote and co-located teams / Susan K. Gerke, Linda V. Berens.-- 1st ed.
    p. cm.
  Summary: "Examines the fundamental aspects of team development with temperament theory-core psychological needs, values, and talents of team members that are essential to the well-being and high performance of a team"--Provided by publisher.
  Includes bibliographical references and index.
  ISBN 0-9719326-0-3 (hardcover)
  1. Teams in the workplace. I. Berens, Linda V. II. Title.
  HD66.G4635 2005
  658.4'022--dc22
                        2005016884

ACKNOWLEDGMENTS

We would like to acknowledge those who have contributed to our knowledge and learning about teams and remote teams as well as those who have contributed specifically to this book. Thank you to those who read early drafts and gave us input. Those people include Tom Edison, Linda Ernst, Bob Gregg, Carol John, Margo Miller, Steve Myers, Brian Robertson, Marci Segal, Karen Shaefer, and Melissa Smith. Thanks to our publisher, Kris Kiler, for asking the tough questions that helped us keep our focus.

Susan and Linda thank each other. We have chosen to write this book together, our second. We are a remote team of two who live 30 miles apart. We meet together for our most collaborative work and then work independently and via e-mail as needed. Our temperament patterns, Rational (Linda) and Guardian (Susan) serve us well as a team. We have learned to use the best of both, to have patience with our differences, and to appreciate what each brings to our work.

Susan would like to acknowledge some people who were key to her learning about teams, teamwork, and remote teamwork:

Steve Hellman, Marilyn Deming, Jan Varney, and I were on a team where we truly learned to work through the Storming stage. It was painful at times, but their feedback and my personal learning have shaped my career and my life in a very positive way.

Dick Richardson, David Hutchens, and I were a truly high performing remote team. We lived in three different states and learned how to work remotely and when to come together for face-to-face work. We invested the time to do all the team development activities that teams should do, and it paid off with an excellent result and great recognition.

My husband, Dave, and I are a team of two. During our twenty-five years together, we've learned a great deal about differences and how to capitalize on those differences rather than let what's different create problems for us. We are a real performing team.

Linda would like to acknowledge those who have helped her understand what teamwork is all about:

In launching the Western Region of the Association for Psychological Type, Louise Giovannoni, Eve Delunas, and Sue Cooper helped set the standard for great teamwork. We had a common goal, did what we did best, discussed our differences using temperament language, and had a great time. Later Art Olguin and I revitalized the organization with some exceptional teamwork.

Linda Ernst and Melissa Smith have served with me as an incredible design team. When Susan joined this team, we welcomed the increased diversity and talent and our teamwork continues to be one of the most satisfying things I do.

I especially appreciate all those clients who have let me inside their team processes to help them improve and then the individuals on those teams who made the efforts to grow so the team could work better together. They have helped prove the value of the *I* in Team.

My husband John and I have faced the challenges of having the same variety of temperament and having to figure out how to cover all the bases needed to run a household and raise two wonderful children. And after forty-one years, the teamwork still works.

CONTENTS

PREFACE

Where Is the *I* in Team?

Many say there is no *I* in Team. We say there is. The *I* stands
for the individual. Teams are made up of individuals who are
expected to work together in a way that produces more than
they could produce working separately. Individuals bring their
talents, goals, role expectations, working habits, and many other
characteristics to the team. They don't suddenly become "we."
There is always a question of, Do I have to give up me to work
effectively on this team? Effective teamwork always is a balanc-
ing act between independence and interdependence, between
the individual and the group. Each individual has core psychological needs, values, and talents that are essential to their well-
being and high performance. Each person is unique, yet each
has many things in common with others.

The *I* is at the core of a team and influences the team. The
unwritten operating guidelines that develop in the team are
greatly influenced by the personality characteristics of the team
members. When the majority of the team share some characteristics, the team can fall into groupthink and not be as resource-
ful and adaptable as it needs to be. If an individual's core
needs are not met, core values are not honored, and talents are
ignored, that team member will not contribute to the synergy

that is possible with teams. Individual differences contribute to increased synergy, but they can also lead to disruptive conflict. Yet most teams jump into doing the assigned work without considering the impact of these individual differences. A lot of diversity on a team creates the potential for much variety in problem solving and for much conflict.

Our experience shows that it's easy to say we want people to work together effectively to achieve the value of great teamwork, but it's not always easy to achieve that great teamwork. High-performing teams (both remote and co-located) spend energy on the development of the team rather than just hoping the team members will achieve success together. We have found it helpful to use frameworks for understanding both the individual and the stages of team development.

The topic of teams and teamwork has been explored in many books over the years. Several elements make this book unique:

- The distinctions we make about remote teamwork to help those who work on remote teams (those on which the members are located in different places)
- The connection we make between team development and personality, specifically temperament
- The insights you will gain about yourself and others that you can use everywhere in your life
- The practical tips we share that can be immediately applied to your team situation

Our experiences with teams and team leaders have shown us that when they use the information in this book, they greatly accelerate team and individual performance as well as improving team satisfaction and quality of work.

Structure of This Book

You may wish to read this book straight through, or you may prefer to use it as a reference. The structure of the book is as follows.

Section I—Setting the Stage
CHAPTER 1—INTRODUCTION AND DEFINITIONS

We clarify terms that are often used interchangeably yet have different meanings. And we define what we mean by remote teamwork.

CHAPTER 2—STAGES OF TEAM DEVELOPMENT

We use the stages of team development as a framework to share teamwork principles and team development techniques.

Section II—A Model for I
CHAPTER 3—IDENTIFYING THE INDIVIDUAL

We use temperament theory to understand individuals better and in turn to understand the dynamics of the team more clearly.

CHAPTER 4—FINDING A BEST-FIT TEMPERAMENT

We describe the four temperaments to help you find a good fit for yourself as well as give you descriptions that will help you understand your teammates.

CHAPTER 5—CLARIFYING YOUR TEMPERAMENT

We give you more explanations of the four temperaments and the things they have in common to help you clarify your own temperament as well as understand things you have in common with others. In addition, we provide you with snapshot descriptions of the four varieties of each temperament to help you sort.

Section III—Integration of the Stages of Team Development and Temperament

CHAPTER 6—FORMING

The Forming stage builds a foundation for the team. Teams that spend productive time in this stage find they can come back to it when they get stuck or are faced with a major change. Investing time in this stage helps teams move forward. We'll look at

- Understanding Temperament and the Forming Stage
- Actions and Tools to Maximize the Forming Stage
- Moving On to the Storming Stage

CHAPTER 7—STORMING

The Storming stage is where teams spend most of their energy. This chapter describes how teams struggle and provides ways to deal with those struggles. We'll look at

- Understanding Temperament and the Storming Stage
- Identifying the Conflicts
- Actions and Tools to Move Through the Storming Stage
- Moving On to the Norming Stage

CHAPTER 8—NORMING

Norming is a stage of productivity. It also is a stage where a team can propel forward into high performance or, if not tended to, can slide back into conflict and frustration. We'll look at

- Understanding Temperament and the Norming Stage
- Actions to Maximize the Norming Stage
- Moving On to the Performing Stage

CHAPTER 9—PERFORMING

Performing is the stage of high performance. Sustaining this level of performance is tough. This chapter gives some tips on maintaining that high level. We'll look at

- Understanding Temperament and the Performing Stage
- Actions to Maximize the Performing Stage
- What to Do When It Ends

Section IV—Special Team Considerations
CHAPTER 10—REMOTE TEAM COMMUNICATION

Remote communication adds additional challenges for teams. This chapter has some tips for meetings and communication among different temperament patterns in remote teams.

CHAPTER 11—EFFECTIVE TEAM LEADERSHIP

While we discuss the leader's role throughout the book, this chapter provides additional focus.

CHAPTER 12—SPECIAL SITUATIONS IN TEAM DEVELOPMENT

Some teams seem to skip stages, some team members seem to find specific stages more appealing and changing membership can affect the team's current stage. This chapter deals with all three special situations

CHAPTER 13—TEAM STRESS

Stress impacts team functioning. Being remote can impact a team member's stress. Also what is stressful for each team member is likely to be influenced by their temperament preference. This chapter explores both remote and temperament stress.

CHAPTER 14—WORKING TOGETHER AND MOVING FORWARD

We summarize the book and make some suggestions for your next steps in making teamwork more productive and satisfying.

The I in TEAM

PART I

SETTING
THE STAGE

INTRODUCTION AND DEFINITIONS

1

Teams and Teamwork

To start the discussion about teams and teamwork, it's useful to tap into our experiences of best team experiences.

Things to think about

Think of the best "team" experience you've ever had. It might have been on a work team, a sports team, a community team—any team that came together to accomplish something. What made your team experience stand out above others you could have chosen?

We find that with this exercise people generally list team characteristics such as the following:

- We trusted each other.
- We had a variety of skills and utilized them well.
- We had a clear, common goal.
- We built on our differences.
- We cared about one another.
- We communicated frequently and well.
- We had good leadership.

Underlying these characteristics and others that we usually hear of is the theme that the successful team paid attention to the interpersonal aspects of their work together. We believe that the interpersonal is key—particularly in remote teams.

Bunches, Groups, and Teams

We've already used the words "team" and "teamwork." Let's do some defining and clarifying.

To begin with, we can look at three ways of people being together. Let's use a bus as a way to compare bunches, groups, and teams.

Suppose you are standing at a bus stop waiting for a bus. And suppose several other people are at the same stop. Each person has his or her own purpose—one may be going shopping, one may be going to work, and another may be going home. This is a bunch. Each person has an individual purpose and the success or failure of each to achieve that purpose is independent of the other people at the bus stop. Teamwork isn't required for bunches.

Now imagine that you are getting on a bus with several colleagues to go to a professional ball game. Suppose one person misses the bus. You have a common purpose—to go to the game—but your ability to accomplish the purpose isn't impacted by the missing person. This is a group.

In the work environment we might relate this example to a department of people who work independently to achieve the department's goals. For example, we might have an accounts payable department where each employee has a specific set of vendors to manage. (Jay has A–I, Jan has J–R, and Jose has S–Z.) If Jay misses a day of work, Jan and Jose can operate just as effectively as if Jay were working. Each person is measured individually and the results are totaled for the group result.

Now let's imagine that we are on the bus on the way to the ball game and the bus skids around a curve and ends up balanced on a high ledge where at any moment it could plunge into a ravine. Any move made by any individual could cause the vehicle to go over the side. Now we are a team. We have a compelling common goal—to survive—and we must work together to solve our problem.

In the workplace, teams are generally organized around a specific project or particular work. The work is integrated in such a way as to create interdependence among team members. And the measurement of results applies to the team as a whole.

In this book, while we are talking about teams, much of the information is also applicable to groups.

In groups and teams, teamwork is important.

Things to think about

Consider a group or team of which you are a member. Is it a group or a team?

What leads you to that conclusion?

The concepts and suggestions in this book apply to both groups and teams. You may find members have a stronger desire to pay attention to these ideas and tips if you are a team versus a group.

Teams, Teaming, and Teamwork

We often use the words "team," "teaming," and "teamwork" interchangeably, yet they really have distinct meanings.

"Team" is a noun. People are assigned to a team and know that they are a member of the team. The definition that we find most useful comes from *The Wisdom of Teams*, by Jon Katzenbach and Douglas Smith:

> *A team is a small number of people with complementary skills who are committed to a common purpose, performance goals, and approach for which they hold themselves mutually accountable.*[1]

"Teaming" is a verb and describes the activities two or more people engage in to do work together. They may be on a formal work team or project team, or they may just need to accomplish something together.

"Teamwork" is a noun that describes how people behave when teaming. It includes behaviors such as the following:

- Sharing information
- Respecting another's point of view
- Giving and receiving feedback
- Making decisions together
- Helping one another

Many people engage in teamwork whether they are on a team or in a group.

Team Development and Team Building

"Team development" and "team building" are two more terms that are often used interchangeably but really have two distinct meanings. Team development is a process that takes place over time to grow a team. It can be an overt process or just the natural process in which a team moves from one stage of development to another. This book is designed to help you with team development.

Team building is generally an event. The event is usually designed either to deal with a problem a team is experiencing (a conflict, the need for process, etc.) or to help team members get to know one another better. Team building events can be very useful to move the team forward, but the idea that a single event will boost a team from low to high performance isn't very realistic. Tools that a team might receive, such as those provided in this book, can extend the effectiveness of a team building event.

Remote Teams

In today's competitive work environment, effective teamwork is a critical factor for success. When people work together, they create opportunities for synergy and creative solutions to problems, giving an organization a competitive edge.

A challenge today that was just a small factor as few as ten to twelve years ago is the increasing number of people working remotely from one another. People who need to work together are spread across buildings, cities, the country, or even the world. Working as a team can be difficult enough without the additional challenge of working physically apart from one another.

Remote working relationships are characterized by the need to schedule time to communicate voice to voice or face to face. The opportunity to "drop in" on each other that exists for co-located teammates doesn't exist in the same way in the remote world. Often, although two workers may work in the same building, when one or both travel extensively they actually have a remote relationship. And with employers being more flexible about employees working at home, some people are remote just because they are working from home on a given day.

Expectations in the workplace have changed. Employees are expected to work effectively with people in other locations whom they may have never met. Technology has enabled workers to work productively from anywhere. However, technology doesn't always account for the human challenges of teamwork. Keeping everyone "in the loop" can be difficult.

Why Talk about Working Remotely?

Is the need to work remotely just a passing phase? Before we decide yes or no, let's look at some of the key factors driving remote work.

First of all, many organizations today are merging or being acquired. When the companies are in different cities (for example, San Diego and Chicago), it is usually more cost effective to keep employees in both locations. Over time, reorganization puts people in the two locations on the same work teams, and the need to work together remotely emerges.

Another driver of remote work can be customers. If your customers demand that you have sales and/or support people located near them, you will find yourself with people working remotely in order to remain competitive.

The growing reluctance of employees to relocate is another driver of the increase in remote relationships. In a two-career family, it may be difficult for both partners to move. Responsibility for aging parents, commitments to the community, reluctance to have children change schools, and so on, can all influence employees to resist relocating.

When an employee has critical skills and tacit company knowledge, companies are often more inclined to respond to some of his or her needs, such as working in a different city or working at home. Rather than lose the employee, companies are willing to set up a remote relationship.

From an economic perspective, relocating people is very expensive for companies. Many companies are also finding they can save money on real estate by having people work from home.

Things to think about

Does your organization use remote workers?

If so, what are the driving factors for this strategy?

If not, why not (industry, organization size, nature of the work, etc.)?

In addition to the driving factors, a number of enablers have resulted in more remote working over the past few years. Technology is a key enabler. The advent and availability of cell phones, laptop computers, fast telephone lines, personal digital assistants, conference calls, video conferences, and collaborative software have made it easy for people to connect from just about anywhere. And the technology just keeps getting better and cheaper, making it easier all the time to work remotely.

Another enabler of remote work is the movement of our society to becoming an information society. Much of what workers need in order to do their jobs is available in company databases or on the Internet. No longer do we have to go to the file cabinets in a central location to find the information we need.

In light of these key drivers and enablers, we think you will agree that working remotely is not just a fad or passing phase. If anything, we're likely to see more of it since it provides some real advantages, such as the following:

- Time to refine written communication so it can be well-thought-out and complete
- Twenty-four hour days for projects to be worked on as they are passed around the world
- Lifestyle improvements for individuals
- Flexibility for organizations
- Opportunities for teams to bring together the best resources for tasks or projects

How Remote is Remote?

Remoteness can have degrees. We can describe four common points on a continuum of remoteness relative to the location of team members.

Co-located   Same Geography   Same Continent   Worldwide

- Co-located—Team members can get together easily. Co-located teams are not remote.
- Same geography—Team members can get together on occasion by driving or walking.
- Same continent—Team members can meet less often. They must use air transportation to get together.
- Worldwide—Team members may never meet face to face.

We can also look at degrees of remoteness relative to time. This range can also be represented by a continuum with four points.

Same Time   Small Time   Large Time   Extreme Time

- Same time—All team members are at work at the same time all the time (same time zone).
- Small time—All team members are at work at the same time some of the time (close time zone differences). There are windows of opportunity to connect.
- Large time—All team members are never at work at the same time (different shifts or distant time zones).
- Extreme time—All team members are never at work at the same time (extreme time zones—probably on different days).

Not Being There

Remoteness can be described as someone "not being there." We have also found aspects of not being there that actually have nothing to do with physical location but have to do with behavior. One situation is where people don't understand the behavior of each other and assume another person isn't "fully present" because his or her response isn't what is expected.

Another situation is where even though co-located, team members don't come out of their offices, and communicate only via e-mail, which creates a sense of not being there that impacts communication and teamwork.

Both kinds of not being there—physically and behaviorally—converge in this book. By looking at team development, remote concerns, and personality differences, we will help you understand what's happening in your team and determine what to do to remedy problems.

Remote Team Challenges and Gripes

When we are on a remote team, we are using something other than face-to-face meetings to interact and accomplish our work.

Remote Team Challenges

Following are some of the most common challenges facing remote team members:

- Getting to know each other
- Learning each other's skills
- Knowing each other's personality and styles
- Clarifying roles
- Spreading the workload
- Building trust
- Solving problems and making decisions
- Resolving conflict

- Keeping everyone updated and involved
- Skillfully using multiple communication vehicles (fax, e-mail, voice mail, collaborative software, conference calls, etc.)

Things to think about

What other challenges is your remote team facing?

What advantages have you found as a remote team?

It turns out that these same challenges often face co-located teams, particularly if the team hasn't focused on them. And remote teamwork has some real advantages.

Remote Team Gripes

Gripes that remote teams often share include the following:

- Timing—having to wait for responses and feeling that others are never available when needed
- Extra effort—driving or flying to other locations for meetings, taking extra time to set up remote meetings, and learning to use special tools
- Expense—paying for conference calls, travel, and special hardware or software to accommodate the remote team
- Miscommunication—missing the nonverbal cues and style differences that are hard to detect remotely

These gripes are easier to live with if the teamwork is good. The same basic teamwork principles apply in both remote and co-located environments, but the techniques can differ. You will find specific tips for the remote environment throughout the book as we give you some frameworks for following basic teamwork principles.

Another Remote Reference

In our first book on the topic of remote work, *Quick Guide to Interaction Styles and Working Remotely* (Gerke and Berens 2003), we included information on the topic of teams but mostly focused on the leadership challenges in working remotely and solutions for those challenges. The following key areas for remote leaders are covered in that book:

- Building remote relationships
- Empowering remote workers, and
- Measuring the performance of remote workers

Remote teamwork issues extend into more areas than we covered previously, and this book will consider those issues as well. You will also see how many teamwork issues are the same whether the team is co-located or remote. We hope you will find this book helpful as you deal with your team issues—both remote and co-located.

STAGES OF
TEAM DEVELOPMENT
2

The four stages of team development, first put forth by Bruce Tuckman and modified and reinforced over the years by many others, provide an excellent structure for looking at the process of developing teams and teamwork. We'll use Tuckman's model as a framework to share teamwork principles and techniques so that you might better understand the impact of these stages on teams you are part of or work with.

In 1974, John Jones expanded on Tuckman's work by examining the stages in a two-dimensional model split between relationship and task. [2]

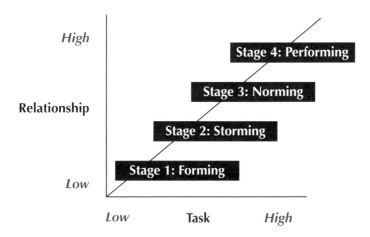

The relationship dimension of the model encompasses all the interrelationships that people experience in teams. The task dimension relates to the functions that the team needs to perform to understand and accomplish its work.

Teams tend to move through the stages sequentially. As a team develops in one stage, it is preparing to move on to the next stage. In order to make the sequential move forward, the team and its leader need to focus and work specifically on their development. In chapters 6, 7, 8, and 9 we describe tasks that will help the team develop in each stage. In part IV, we provide further thoughts on the movement of the team.

Stage 1: Forming

The characteristics of the first stage, Forming, are as follows:
- Some excitement, anticipation, and optimism
- Some anxiety: Where do I fit?
- Expectation: looking to the leader for guidance and direction
- Politeness among team members
- Caution
- Need of individuals to find a place and establish themselves

Questions individuals ask themselves in this stage include the following:
- What's our purpose?
- What will my role be?
- Who are these other people?
- How will we work together?

Characteristics of Forming tend to fit with Richard Beckhard's model of the team's need to establish goals, roles, norms and relationships.[3] You will notice an emphasis on each of these key areas throughout this book.

In remote teams, the needs that people have in this stage are often ignored, dooming the team to member frustration if not team failure. The most preferred way to satisfy the needs of the Forming stage is to bring the team together and spend time on the key elements. That is not always an option for remote teams and may need to be done via teleconference, Web conference, or some other means. We'll share ways to handle each element of the Forming stage in both a face-to-face and a remote interaction.

Stage 2: Storming

The characteristics of the second stage, Storming, are as follows:

- Discrepancy between hopes and reality
- Disagreement about goals, tasks, and action plans
- Lack of progress toward goals
- Feelings of incompetence and confusion
- Competition for power and attention
- Formation of subgroups
- Scapegoating
- Resistance to being led
- Miscommunication
- Unresolved conflicts

The name of this stage, "Storming," gives an idea of what goes on during this stage of development. Storming can manifest itself in a variety of ways:

- Continued politeness in meetings followed by side conversations in subgroups about problems
- Verbal confrontations
- Quiet undermining of the team and team leadership

Remote teams might show Storming in:

- E-mail exchanges
- "Unavailability" of members
- Side conversations in "instant messaging"

Storming is an interesting stage. We've found that when a team reaches this stage, it has four options:

1. The team will be reorganized.

It will be determined that this isn't the "right team" of people and concluded that a different combination of people will be more successful.

Of course, when the new team is formed, it will also move to the Storming stage. Behaviors might look different, but the team will still go through the Storming stage.

2. The team will become a "do good" team.

If the team has an unspoken conflict about relationships (personality conflicts, style differences, not liking someone) the team will focus on doing the work individually. You'll hear members saying, "I did my part" or "It didn't go wrong on my watch," and you will not see members help one another. Such teams are very common in organizations. They are often allowed to continue because they produce work.

The problem, however, is that the quality of the work is generally lower than it could be. Without input from multiple people, the team will have fewer ideas to select from and therefore lower potential for solutions. Allowing "do good" teams to operate is a going-out-of-business strategy.

3. The team will become a "feel good" team.

The unspoken conflict for this type of team is about how to do the work or what work to focus on. However, members truly like each other. You will see team members having lunch together, sharing personal information, and even spending time together outside the work environment, but you won't see them discussing or engaging in work.

This team is generally found out and disbanded pretty quickly since the team doesn't accomplish work.

Susan was once on a "feel good" remote team. The team of ten members spread across the western United States got together quarterly for a three-day meeting. Team members really enjoyed each other's company and had a great time eating out and attending special events together such as a ball game and the circus. During the daytime meetings, however, each new topic was met with a variety of opinions on how to deal with it. When conflict emerged, the leader quickly moved on to the next subject, so that the team made no decisions and accomplished little or no actual work together. In less than a year, the team was disbanded.

4. The team will work through the conflict.

This is the best option if you want high performance and high quality results. In fact, differences (conflict) can be positive in a team if the team members can work together to resolve those differences. Leading the team through the conflict is generally the role of the leader. We'll share more later on how to do this.

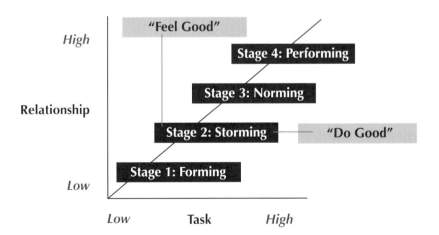

Dealing with the Storming stage can be particularly difficult for remote teams since conflict most likely cannot be resolved face to face.

Stage 3: Norming

The characteristics of the third stage, Norming, are as follows:
- Feelings of relief and confidence
- A sense of team cohesion
- Development of harmony, trust, support, and respect
- Acknowledgment of member contributions
- Evidence of real progress toward goals
- More openness and feedback
- Use of team language

It's usually a relief for a team to reach this stage. The members have survived Storming and can move forward together. The members now know what to expect from one another, they are giving and receiving feedback without getting defensive, and most important, real work is being accomplished.

A concern at this stage is that the team will be satisfied with these changes and not strive to move on to the next stage, where true synergy happens.

Remote teams can be very effective at this stage, but need to take time to stay connected.

Stage 4: Performing

The characteristics of the fourth stage, Performing, are as follows:
- A feeling of pride
- Increased output and higher quality work
- Shared responsibility
- Collaboration of the whole team and of subgroups

- Close connection of the team members
- Adjusted roles based on the needs of the team
- Spontaneously emerging leadership
- Shared leadership
- High levels of performance

The Performing stage is the ultimate goal, yet many teams never reach this stage. Reasons might include the following:

- Change in the goal
- Change in team membership
- Change in leadership
- Completion of the task or project

However, this stage is so satisfying that once you've been on a performing team, you have a hunger to achieve this level again.

Remote performing teams don't find their remoteness to be a concern or a limiting factor. Their teamwork transcends the challenges of distance and time.

What Stage Is Your Team Experiencing?

Review the characteristics listed in the assessment tables below and place a check next to those items that are true for your team.

Stage 1: Forming Characteristics	True for My Team
Some excitement, anticipation, and optimism	
Some anxiety: Where do I fit?	
Expectation: Looking to the leader for guidance and direction	
Politeness among team members	
A cautious atmosphere	
Need in individuals to find a place and establish themselves	

See Chapter 6 for more information on Forming Characteristics

STAGE 2: STORMING CHARACTERISTICS	TRUE FOR MY TEAM
Discrepancy between hopes and reality	
Disagreement about goals, tasks, and action plans	
Lack of progress toward goals	
Feelings of incompetence and confusion	
Competition for power and attention	
Formation of subgroups	
Scapegoating	
Resistance to being led	
Miscommunication	
Unresolved conflicts	

See Chapter 7 for more information on Storming Characteristics

STAGE 3: NORMING CHARACTERISTICS	TRUE FOR MY TEAM
Feelings of relief and confidence	
A sense of team cohesion	
Development of harmony, trust, support, and respect	
Acknowledgment of member contributions	
Evidence of real progress toward goals	
More openness and feedback	
Use of team language	

See Chapter 8 for more information on Norming Characteristics

Stage 4: Performing Characteristics	True for My Team
A feeling of pride	
Increased output and quality of work	
Shared responsibility	
Collaboration by the whole team and by subgroups	
Close connection of the team members	
Adjustment of roles based on the needs of the team	
Spontaneously emerging leadership	
Shared leadership	
High levels of performance	

See Chapter 9 for more information on Performing Characteristics

If you have checks in any of the four assessments, we suggest you read the appropriate chapter ("Forming," Chapter 6; "Storming," Chapter 7; "Norming," Chapter 8; or "Performing," Chapter 9) to learn strategies to help your team develop appropriately. For example, even if you have only one check in the Forming assessment, you need to address the Forming issues before the Storming issues. Each of the chapters builds on the information about temperament in chapters 4 and 5. Even if you are already familiar with temperament theory, you may find it worthwhile to revisit this information.

Team Leadership

The team's leader has an important role at each stage of development. Broadly speaking, the leader's role at each stage is

Forming—Provide direction

Storming—Facilitate the team

Norming—Let go

Performing—Get out of the way

When a team doesn't have a formal leader, someone will have to take on the leadership role for the Forming and Storming stages or the team is likely to flounder. Some leaderless teams deal with this challenge by assigning different aspects of the leader role to individual team members. For example, someone will clarify roles, someone will clarify goals, someone will make sure people get to know each other, and so on. As we explore each stage we will discuss in depth what the team needs from the leader and what it needs to do for itself.

Because every team is made up of individuals, before we go into more depth on the team and how to deal with the stages, it's useful to understand more about the individuals. We believe the temperament model presented here is a useful way to do that. [4]

PART II

A
MODEL
FOR I

IDENTIFYING
THE INDIVIDUAL

3

Groups and teams are made up of individuals, and so cooperation is required for good teamwork. One of the major issues a team faces is that every team member has to deal with the question, Do I have to give up me to be a part of this team? This issue of individual identity and how it fits with the team is best dealt with by using a good framework for looking at personality differences on the team. It all starts with understanding yourself and understanding others.

We typically expect others to behave and think just the way we do. Therefore, differences are often the source of conflict on teams. They can also be a source of synergy. We have found that having a common language with which to talk about those differences helps bridge the gap between destructive conflict and synergistic high performance.

Classifying Individual Differences [5]

As people seek to understand individual differences, they tend to gravitate toward classification systems. Having some ways to organize and simply understand the complexities of human behavior is very helpful.

When trying to understand personality, it is important to recognize that all we have to go on is the outer behavior we observe. Much like in the following picture, all we see are shadows.

If we assume what is behind the behavior, we may misunderstand the true nature of that individual's personality. As we can see, we might expect a sphere to have made these shadows, but if the light is right, several other shapes can make the same shape shadow.

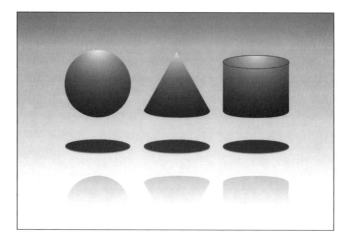

So when an organizational setting requires or sets a norm for certain behaviors, individuals of different personality types may exhibit very similar behaviors.

Personality Has Several Aspects

Just as our behavior is not determined by our personality type, the cylinder can have a rectangular shadow or an oval shadow depending on how the light is shining.

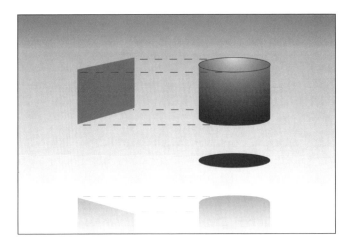

All behavior occurs in a context— be it work, school, home, socializing, and so on. It is important to understand that our personalities reflect the requirements of these contexts as well as our innate tendencies and how we have adapted to these contexts over time.

The Contextual Self

The contextual self is who we are in any given environment. It is how we behave depending on what the situation requires. The idea of a personality "type" doesn't leave out freedom of action in the moment.

The Developed Self

When the contextual self becomes habitual and ongoing, it becomes a part of your developed self. Personality development is influenced by our choices and decisions as well as by interactions and roles.

The Core Self

This aspect of our personality exists from the beginning of our lives. This aspect of ourselves is in our genes. We are born with a tendency to behave in certain ways, which influences how we adapt, grow, and develop.

When we look at ourselves on a team, all three of these aspects must be considered. Current behavior and adaptations may or may not be consistent with the core self. All are interrelated.

As you explore the framework presented here, try to sort out what is at your core. We have found it most effective when people are aware of their core selves even though they choose to behave in ways that are not in alignment with that core. In fact, we've found that adaptability increases once people get the sense of freedom that comes from finding a good fit with who they are naturally.

What is Temperament Theory [6]

Temperament theory is a systemic approach to understanding patterns in human behavior. Temperament patterns describe ways in which human personalities interact with the environment to satisfy needs.

Temperament theory provides answers to questions like these: What motivates group members to move forward? What roles do members naturally assume? What are the core needs of members in groups? What are the innate talents of group members? What are the typical behaviors you can expect to see in group members?

The purpose of using temperament theory to understand the psychology of group members is to provide a language and a vehicle by which the groups can improve their functioning.

A Little History

Ancient Greek and classical German writers and psychologists developed the concept of temperament. Hippocrates, Paracelsus, Ernst Kretschmer, and Eduard Spranger each perceived the human species as a total system, seeking survival in four different and complementary ways.[7]

David Keirsey, a modern psychologist, was inspired by these thought leaders.[8] Linda Berens, a former student of Keirsey's and director of TRI (formerly Temperament Research Institute), has built on and made his work more accessible, understandable, practical, and meaningful for use by individuals in teams.[9]

What You Need to Know about Temperament Theory [10]

1. Temperament demonstrates a system of human behavior apparent in four specific and unique patterns.
2. Temperament drives behavior. Your activities cluster into patterns that organize around meeting your temperament needs and core values.
3. Temperament governs how you grow and how you adapt to meet your needs.
4. Temperament is inborn. It is revealed through themes that originate from your core values. You, your colleagues, and your children each have one of the four temperaments as a theme that drives behavior.
5. Your temperament remains constant through your life. It unfolds over time as does your physical, emotional, spiritual, and psychological development.
6. Your temperament pattern energy is best expressed when your core needs are met through acting from your associated core values.

7. Stress occurs when your core needs are not being met. Stress also appears when the values associated with your needs are not being honored or expressed or are repressed.
8. You have a predisposition for one of the four temperaments' themes. This one theme directs your adaptation to the environment and the people in it. As you develop, you also learn and use coping strategies and skills associated with other temperament themes to meet your need for survival in your context—at work, at home, and so on.

Understanding Yourself and Others through Self-Discovery [11]

Self-Reflection

The Johari Window, originally used for improving communication, is a useful map to help us understand how we can better find out more about ourselves and others.[12]

For example, there is "public knowledge"—things we know about ourselves and that are known to others around us. These public aspects of ourselves are easily recognized. What do we talk about over coffee or around the water cooler? Discovering how we communicate in general is one part of getting in touch with who we really are. Listen to what you say and how you say it. What are the kinds of subjects you like to talk about? These subjects will likely reflect your natural self. Be aware that your public self may reflect adaptive or learned behavior. This adaptive self is also part of who you are but may not hold the key to what energizes you.

Public knowledge contributes to good team functioning since it is hard to talk about information that is not shared. And information that is clearly understood is easier to communicate. So it is important for you to learn about yourself and to share some of that information with others.

The Johari Window

	Known to Self	Unknown to Self
Known to Others	**Public Knowledge...** *What I show you*	**Feedback...** *Your gift to me*
Unknown to Others	**Private...** *Mine to share*	**Unconscious...** *Not to Probe but I can become more aware and choose to share*

Interaction with Others: Sharing and Feedback

We also learn who we are through our interactions with others. Finding people who are similar to us and comparing notes and sharing stories helps many of us find our own best-fit temperament pattern. This process often happens in workshops when people openly discuss their temperaments in order to better understand themselves and others. Sometimes this kind of discussion takes us into the "private" area of the Johari Window—those aspects known to ourselves and not known to others. In the same way, self-discovery often sends us to this area, at least privately.

One valuable way of finding out who we are is by actively seeking feedback—asking others to tell us how they see us. These people may be trained facilitators or merely people who know us well. The "feedback" area of the Johari Window gives us the opportunity to learn about those aspects of ourselves unknown to us but known to others. This provides additional information as we explore who we are. And remember, this feedback is a gift, often given through the eyes of the giver—so seek feedback from many people.

On teams, giving feedback is important. Understanding more about the person you are giving feedback to helps you deliver your message so it is well received rather than rejected. Use the information you gain from this chapter to help you understand others and what is important to them as well as to understand yourself. Then apply that knowledge to giving feedback.

Openness to New Information

During the process of self-discovery, "unconscious" information sometimes comes into our minds—aspects previously unknown to ourselves and unknown to others. In the temperament model, the unconscious is often where we store information about how to "be" in the world. As you explore who you are, stay open to valuable insights from this area.

Many variables may affect your self-discovery process. Be aware that family, social, cultural, and other influences will affect how you view yourself in relation to the temperament patterns. These influences are often unconscious until they come into our awareness when they are described and pointed out. Stay open and searching. Seek input from all areas of the Johari Window.

FINDING A BEST-FIT TEMPERAMENT

4

There are many ways to find your own best-fit temperament pattern. There are personality instruments that can point you to the pattern that is likely to fit you, yet we've found the most powerful way is to follow the self-discovery method recommended in chapter 3 using good narrative descriptions. If you have used an instrument that gave you temperament results, then use the following descriptions to verify those results. Keep in mind that the instruments are not always accurate. If you are new to this framework, use the descriptions to find a good fit for yourself. You can get feedback from people who know you well to augment your experience.

A Quick Look at the Four Temperaments

First, each of the four temperament patterns is described with a snapshot that gives a quick look at the pattern. You may find a good fit just by reading the snapshots. If so, we encourage you to read the full description of your preferred temperament pattern. If the snapshots aren't enough for you to discern your best-fit pattern, then you will find the rest of this chapter useful.

The Artisan Temperament
ARTISANS...

Want the freedom to choose the next act. Seek to have impact, to get results. Want to be graceful, bold, and impressive. Generally are excited and optimistic. Are absorbed in the action of the moment. Are oriented toward the present. Seek adventure and stimulation. Hunger for spontaneity. Trust impulses, luck, and their ability to solve any problem they run into. Think in terms of variation. Have the ability to notice and describe rich detail, constantly seeking relevant information. Like freedom to move, festivities, and games. Are natural negotiators. Seize opportunities. Are gifted tacticians, deciding the best move to make in the moment, the expedient action to take. Are frequently drawn to all kinds of work that requires variation on a theme.

SOUND LIKE YOU? READ MORE ON PAGE 38

The Guardian Temperament
GUARDIANS...

Want to fit in, to have membership. Hunger for responsibility, accountability, and predictability. Tend to be generous, to serve, and to do their duty. Establish and maintain institutions and standard operating procedures. Tend to protect and preserve, to stand guard and warn. Look to the past and tradition. Foster enculturation with ceremonies and rules. Trust contracts and authority. Want security and stability. Think in terms of what is conventional, comparisons, associations, and discrete elements. Generally are serious and concerned, fatalistic. Are skilled at ensuring that things, information, and people are in the right place, in the right amounts, in the right quality, at the right time. Frequently gravitate toward business and commerce.

SOUND LIKE YOU? READ MORE ON PAGE 43

Rational Temperament
RATIONALS...

Want knowledge and to be competent, to achieve. Seek to understand how the world and things in it work. Are theory oriented. See everything as conditional and relative. Are oriented to the infinite. Trust logic and reason. Want to have a rationale for everything. Are skeptical. Think in terms of differences, delineating categories, definitions, structures, and functions. Hunger for precision, especially in thought and language. Are skilled at long-range planning, inventing, designing, and defining. Generally are calm. Foster individualism. Frequently gravitate toward technology and the sciences. Are well suited for engineering and devising strategy, whether in the social or physical sciences.

SOUND LIKE YOU? READ MORE ON PAGE 48

Idealist Temperament
IDEALISTS...

Want to be authentic, benevolent, and empathic. Search for identity, meaning, and significance. Are relationship oriented, particularly valuing meaningful relationships. Are romantic and idealistic, wanting to make the world a better place. Look to the future. Trust their intuition, imagination, impressions. Focus on developing potential, fostering and facilitating growth through coaching, teaching, counseling, communicating. Generally are enthusiastic. Think in terms of integration and similarities and look for universals. Are gifted in the use of metaphors to bridge different perspectives. Are diplomatic. Frequently are drawn to work that inspires and develops people and relationships.

SOUND LIKE YOU? READ MORE ON PAGE 53

Temperament Descriptions

If the snapshots didn't clarify your preferred temperament pattern, use the following more-detailed descriptions. Each starts with a portrait that describes the pattern from the outside in. This section will help you learn about others. Then each description presents a self-portrait that is written in the language of that temperament from a first person point of view. This will help you "try-on" the pattern to see if it fits.

The Artisan Temperament

For the Artisan, life is a process of making instantaneous decisions among an array of options.

Born with a predisposition for keen observation of the specific and the concrete in the present moment, Artisans tend to focus on the immediate and to be captured by whatever is happening and do whatever is expedient. They excel at astute observation of human behavior and are skilled at seizing opportunities and predicting the moves others will make in the short run. They often are skillful in crisis and emergency situations, able to see exactly what's needed and respond with whatever is at hand, without the concerns for competence or propriety that might inhibit other types. Such a focus gives them a talent for improvisation, fitting pieces together, blending, meshing, and remodeling. They are masters at variation, both for the fun of it and for practical problem solving.

Artisans value freedom and pragmatism above all else. As a result, they often appear to avoid ties, plans, commitments, or obligations that can get in the way of being spontaneous. This enables them to be tolerant and easygoing in most situations and often to rely on the situation itself to structure their time and responses. Because of their adaptability, they can often behave like chameleons and respond to the behavioral cues from any type of person in any situation. Their pragmatic perspective leads them to do whatever is useful in order to get the greatest result with the least effort. And yet they may devote a lot of time and effort to achieving perfection in whatever is theirs to achieve. Their power orientation expresses itself in proceeding to action, thereby taking control of a situation.

In an energetic mood, Artisans crave activity and the freedom to act on the needs of the moment in a spontaneous way. Dull routine and structure put them to sleep or force them to "act out" if they cannot escape. They prefer activities with an immediate or near-term payoff or those that impact themselves or others. The payoff or impact can be tangible or take the form of feelings of risk for themselves or others. Since Artisans are the ultimate pragmatists, everything, including people, theories, and ideas, can be tools for reaching the exhilaration that comes with the execution of a perfect act, an act full of grace, dexterity, or finesse.

Artisans are apt to show a cool exterior, masking a general mood of excitement. They seek autonomy, tactical one-upsmanship, and competition in social situations and adopt a fraternal camaraderie with those who play with them on the "team."

Often Artisans insist on negotiation over objects or issues. Their basic cynical point of view appears to be that "people are only in it for what they can get out of it." Although generally optimistic, they are not disillusioned when people act in their own interest rather than for the common good.

Artisans place a high value on competence that shows in actual performance and is not just claimed by a degree or by position. They most admire people of great skill, the cool or flamboyant virtuoso, hero, high roller, adventurer, inventor, and so on. They despise awkwardness, meekness, and cowardliness, such as that found in "stool pigeons" and "chickens." Their chief internal enemy is boredom. They are stressed by wordiness, abstraction, uneventful routine, restraint, and lockstep procedure. They do their best in an open atmosphere or a loosely structured one that affords competition, freedom, opportunity, variation, and change. They love helping people by problem solving, fixing things, and making things happen.

They are a culture's foremost tacticians. They focus on what can be done now to achieve impossible goals.

Self-Portrait of the Artisan Temperament

As an Artisan...

I must be doing something. I cannot tolerate being bored and I get bored easily. Wherever I am, I find something to do. I need variety and stimulation. It is important that I have freedom. Any situation that is confining will make me miserable, and I will do whatever it takes to change confining circumstances. I love to make an impact and to do the unpredictable. I live for this moment; the past is gone and the future will take care of itself. I want to squeeze the most I can out of life.

I am very adaptable and take great pride in doing many different things. I am often described as a chameleon because I fit into so many different contexts. I have my own style and do my own thing, but I know how to play the game of life. I love a challenge and will often do something just to prove that I can. I want to prove it to others, but it is even more important to prove it to myself.

I like things to look good in an aesthetic sense. I am very aware of my surrounding environment, and anything that detracts from a setting spoils the whole experience for me. I have a natural sense of style and composition, and I know when something lacks a pleasing quality. It doesn't have to be beautiful, just aesthetically fluid.

I believe I can do anything if I have the opportunity to try. I learn best by doing, not studying. I like to jump right in and start a project. I work best when I can start with one approach and then change or vary it to suit the situation better. I am likely to do things no one else has thought of or dared to try. I am great at finding a way to meet a goal. Usually it is not the conventional way, but it is expeditious and effective. It gets the job done!

I am in my element when there is a crisis or problem to be solved. Leave me alone so I can get to it and in no time I have the situation under control. I seem to instinctively know just what to do. I quickly assess the situation and act; it is not a long, contemplative process. I just do it naturally. I can sense opportunity in my gut, and when I respond I am usually right on target. When I neglect my instincts I usually pay a price.

I am impressed when people are really skilled at something, and I love it when people notice my skills. I have "tool intelligence." I seem to know how things operate, and I have the dexterity to make them work well, whether I'm driving a car, flipping pancakes, or setting the VCR. I am rarely clumsy, and I consciously work on my own individual style and presence.

Sometimes people think I am frivolous and irresponsible. On the contrary, I am serious about enjoying life in all of its capacities. I do have fun, but I also set goals and challenges for myself and work hard to achieve them. I have strong personal convictions, but I don't impose them on others, and I don't respond positively when others impose their convictions on me. I only appear irresponsible when I am in a confining situation; in an attempt to free myself of the trapped feeling, I may sometimes let others down. But I have learned to maintain commitments by incorporating some sense of freedom into the agreements I make with others. I am reliable and loyal when my freedom is not compromised. I will test the limits of others, but I do have a keen sense of just how far I can go before I jeopardize a relationship.

I am interested in what other people want because that knowledge makes it easy for me to interact with them. I love to make an impact on people, and when I know what strikes a chord with them I can quickly move our interaction along. I am good at knowing what to say and when to say it.

WHAT I NEED FROM OTHERS

I need others to give me space. I enjoy people, but I find too many expectations confining. I want to do things, not just think or talk about them. I want to be appreciated for my troubleshooting talents by being relieved of constraints on my freedom when there is no crisis. I want my free-spirit approach to be seen as a viable and responsible way to live life.

HOW OTHERS PERCEIVE ME

Other people see me as fun, quick, and a risktaker. They believe things come to me easily and that I am lucky. They often see me as a maverick or free spirit. They think I am a lot of fun to be around, but they want me to prove that I am reliable.

Essential Qualities of the Artisan Temperament
NEEDS AND VALUES

The Artisan's core needs are to have the freedom to act without hindrance and to see a marked result from action. Artisans highly value aesthetics, whether in nature or in art. Their energies are focused on skillful performance, variety, and stimulation. They tend toward pragmatic, utilitarian actions with a focus on technique. They trust their impulses and have a drive to action. Artisans learn best experientially and when they see the relevance of what they are learning to what they are doing. They enjoy hands-on, applied learning with a fast pace and freedom to explore.

TALENTS

Artisans tend to be gifted at employing the available means to accomplish an end. Their creativity is revealed by the variety of solutions they come up with. They are talented at using tools, whether the tool be language, theories, a paint brush, or a computer. Artisans tune in to immediate sensory information and vary their actions according to the needs of the moment. They are gifted at tactics. They can easily read the situation at hand, instantly make decisions, and, if needed, take actions to achieve the desired outcome.

The Guardian Temperament

For the Guardian, life is a process of responsibly cultivating and preserving resources and relationships.

Guardians are born with a predisposition for observing and preserving the concrete "realities" of the present. Those "realities" may be rituals, rites, traditions, conventions, manners, facts, relationships, material, institutions, or life itself. Their focus is on the present and the past and how to improve what exists without losing the best from days gone by. With such a focus, Guardians excel at noticing when something required or agreed upon is not done and then following up to make sure it happens. Regulatory activities within society, such as conserving, policing, guarding, counting, stabilizing, and ritualizing, often come under their jurisdiction. They recognize that establishing and articulating the rules, sanctions, standard operating procedures, timelines, predictable routines, and protocol makes things easier for people and institutions.

Above all others, Guardians value the presence of order, lawfulness, security, propriety, bonds, and contracts. Activities that foster these principles keep life simple and ensure the continuance of the world as it is known. Likewise, the virtues of dependability, responsibility, obedience, compliance, and cooperation are necessary in their world, as these virtues add up to everyone contributing his or her fair share to the common good. As those who tend to make constant comparisons, Guardians are often concerned about everyone carrying a fair portion of the load for benefits received. Their power orientation is expressed in adherence to roles and support of the groups to which they belong.

Guardians can frequently portray a mood of concern. While they see themselves as optimistic, the unknowns of the future invariably disrupt their world and give them plenty of experiences that can sometimes foster a pessimistic point of view. They turn their logistical talents to preparing for the worst so the best can happen.

Guardians seek affiliation within hierarchies and social structures with clearly defined roles, responsibilities, and lines of authority. These structures provide security and pose the least threat of disruption to a system. From the Guardians' point of view, it is nice to know one can get the work done without disruption and, therefore, earn one's reward in a stable world.

Guardians like to be included in what's going on. Thus, they find membership in family, groups, and organizations satisfying. They often view organizations as either families or armies united for some useful purpose. This can lead to Guardians taking maternal, paternal, or authoritative roles in relation to others.

Guardians admire those with common sense, as well as those with legitimate authority, empowered by degrees, position, divine right, or hard work. A particular favorite is the person who worked his or her way up through the ranks, pulling their fair weight all the way.

Abandonment, exclusion, disrespect for authority, dereliction, and disobedience, all of which threaten the common bond, are particularly offensive and stressful to Guardians. They do their best when allowed to take on responsibility and when given appreciation and direction from authority. Guardians can demonstrate an incredible capacity for constancy, caretaking and achievement in such an atmosphere.

The Guardians are a culture's foremost overseers and providers and seek to support families, work groups, schools, government, and all kinds of organizations to ensure continuity.

Self-Portrait of the Guardian Temperament

As a Guardian…

I am first and foremost a responsible person. I believe it is important for all of us to contribute to society as best we can so things will run as smoothly as possible. I have a strong sense of duty and loyalty to my family, friends, colleagues, and community. It is important for me and the people close to me to be safe and comfortable.

I am constantly aware of all of the tasks that need to be done, and I feel uncomfortable if things are not getting accomplished. I tend to stick to a schedule and familiar routines so I am certain to fit everything into my day. I spend much of my time making sure other people have all they need to be comfortable or to accomplish their tasks. Sometimes I get overwhelmed by all of the work I must get done, especially when others assume I will do things and don't ask me if I have the time. It is difficult for me to ask for help, but I am learning to say no to some requests.

I have many roles in my life that influence what I do. I pay attention to how people are related to one another in terms of history, hierarchy, experiences, and types of relationships. It is clear to me that my roles come with particular responsibilities, norms, and standards of appropriate behavior. I am offended and disappointed when people show disrespect for my roles or do not live up to the responsibilities of their own roles. We all have roles to play in the grand scheme of things; that is what keeps the world going.

I rely on my past experiences to guide me. I am always looking for the best, most efficient ways to do tasks. I can barely tolerate waste. I believe that there is a "tried and true" way to do a job and that to do it differently defies common sense. I know lots of how-to's and how-not-to's that can save time and energy.

I tend to appreciate family and cultural traditions. I have many stories of family, friends, and colleagues and rich remembrances of times we have spent together. Life's milestones of birth, graduation, marriage, promotion, retirement, and death are important events I acknowledge and participate in as a means of maintaining my relationships. It is also important to other people that I be there to support them in these significant moments.

I believe it is important to be prepared, to work hard, and to be helpful to others. I prefer to have things planned out in advance so I can avoid negative consequences. I dislike surprises, and I do not like changing a plan just for the sake of change. If there is truly a more efficient way of doing something, I want to be shown; otherwise, I am going to stick to what I have done in the past. I expect others to keep their word and act responsibly. I value accomplishments, so I like to be able to focus on a task until it is complete. I am generally thorough and have a clear sense of the beginning, middle, and end of a project.

I need a clear description of what is expected of me, the desired goal, a suggested procedure, the available resources, and the chain of command anytime there is a task or project for me to do. One of my natural skills is putting stabilizing structures in place that will make things easier. I develop new procedures by comparing new tasks to tasks I have done in the past. I am good at demonstrating how things are done so others can learn from my experience. I believe in earning my accomplishments through hard work, diligence, and effort. Often my contributions go unnoticed by others, when a simple thank-you would increase my morale considerably.

WHAT I NEED FROM OTHERS

I need to be appreciated for the simple ways I support others day to day. A sincere thank-you or a special gesture that will make things easier for me goes a long way. I like to be asked to be included in projects and events even though I may not always have time to participate. When people follow through on commitments to me and fulfill their responsibilities in a timely manner, it is more than a courtesy; it demonstrates their respect for me. I love it when people ask for my experience and support.

HOW OTHERS PERCEIVE ME

Other people see me as organized, courteous, responsible, and loyal. They know I am someone they can count on to help out in whatever way I can. Sometimes people think I am too structured and organized and not spontaneous enough. People generally describe me as a good student, spouse, parent, friend, or coworker.

Essential Qualities of the Guardian Temperament
NEEDS AND VALUES

The Guardian's core needs are for group membership and responsibility. Guardians need to know they are doing the responsible thing. They value stability, security, and a sense of community. They trust hierarchy and authority and may be surprised when others go against these social structures. Guardians prefer cooperative actions with a focus on standards and norms. Their orientation is to their past experiences and they like things sequenced and structured. Guardians tend to look for the practical applications of what they are learning.

TALENTS

Guardians are usually talented at logistics and at maintaining useful traditions. They masterfully get the right things in the right place, at the right time, in the right quantity, in the right quality, to the right people and not to the wrong people. Guardians know how things have always been done, and so they anticipate where things can go wrong. They have a knack for attending to rules, procedures, and protocol. They make sure the correct information is assembled and presented to the right people.

The Rational Temperament

For the Rational, life is a process of acquiring knowledge and competencies for their own sake or for the political, pragmatic, or strategic advantage such knowledge can give an individual or group.

Born with a predisposition for the complex, Rationals tend to focus on patterns and "think systems," both technical and social, and move with ease from the big picture to the minute details of ideas or situations. With such a versatile focus, they often excel at design, schematizing, reasoning, strategizing, analysis, synthesis, forecasting, trend analysis, logic, and problem solving. They are adept at seeing the basic principles and unformed possibilities, which leads to visioning and inventing. They are among the world's chief innovators, some driven to implementation of the visions and others driven to designs.

Rationals place a high value on competence, coherence, and quality. They engage in activities primarily because they might learn from them, rather than for deep significance, for duty, or for enjoyment. Their power orientation expresses itself in a search for strategic advantage.

The Rationals' prevailing mood is one of tranquility. They seek to identify and solve problems and enigmas. Sometimes their absorption in the abstract or the future can lead them to seem distant or aloof. They are often competitive and independent and appear to have little regard for common bonds. Bonding for them comes in the form of a shared interest or project. When in a nurturing role, they tend to focus on the competence and intellectual development of those whom they contact.

Rationals come into a situation with an almost immediate understanding of the overall system, how it functions, and the factors at work. There are always many factors and levels to consider, often with no easy, or at least no easily articulated, answers. Figuring out a system's specifics is often perceived as time better spent elsewhere. Learning means understanding the process of learning, and Rationals are constantly searching for knowledge that is abstract yet explicit. This gives them the power to act in a logical, more objective way that is still tailored to a goal or situation. When a field of study is thoroughly digested, Rationals can explain how they know what they know, when they knew it, and how that knowledge can be extended. Figuring something out means finding more to explore at a deeper level, with their eagerness to explore new or controversial areas tempered by the need for verification, proof, or performance. They cannot help but play with ideas and test them. With expertise, Rationals can introduce radical and insightful changes with ease. Rationals appear naturally curious. With their analytical and skeptical point of view, they can find themselves doubting anything and everything. Rationals have a high tolerance for complexity and are often surprised by others' resistances to problem solving. Their independence of thought leads to a need for autonomy in the workplace.

They most admire will power and genius, the wizards and inventors of the world, and they despise redundancy, incompetence, and weak will. They are their own worst critics and are often stressed by a fear of incompetence, loss of control, and helplessness. Rigid, routine, dull environments offend them and may drive them away. They do their best in situations that stimulate them intellectually and that allow them to have control over their learning and expression of their ideas. They can enjoy being challenged and critiqued on their own ground, taking such constructive criticisms as evidence that the critic has truly understood their project.

They are a culture's foremost visionaries and pioneers and seek to contribute their strategy, design, and invention.

Self-Portrait of the Rational Temperament

As a Rational…

I am a perpetual learner. I am constantly in search of answers—fundamental truths—to help me improve and to achieve, and I am never completely satisfied with the answers because there are always more complexities, more questions to explore, and more avenues for progress. Logic and reason are mainstays. I am interested in the logic behind logic and the thinking behind thinking. I want to know why things are the way they are and why things work the way they do. I have a natural inclination to create or launch something that has never been done and enter unknown territory.

I am a natural systems thinker looking for leverage points in the system. I notice what others asume in everyday life and question the premise and merit of each assumption. I have a sense that humanity is destined to promote progress. I have an inherent understanding of "natural law" and use that knowledge to consider and improve the way things are done. Elegant ideas and theories that explain the aesthetic beauty of natural law can offer a lifetime of stimulation. Elegance elicits efficiency and precision in a system, changing and improving its quality in a way that often goes unrecognized by society.

Self-mastery is a motivating force in my life. I set my own standards, which are undoubtedly high, and achieve them. I do not rely on others for appraisal of my work, but I do like to be acknowledged for innovative contributions. My work is my play; I have fun while challenging myself. Expertise and full knowledge of a profession or area of interest are very important. I aspire to be precise in all things, particularly in defining ideas and how I think of the words that express them.

Incompetence is my nemesis. It makes me feel stupid and like a failure. To avoid it, I strive for competency in all that I do. My strategy is to understand the underlying principles, the inherent assumptions, and the methodology behind what I do so I can improve my capabilities. I will continuously improve my skills, striving for perfection—perfection, in my mind, being the highest level at which I can achieve my intended purpose.

Problem solving comes naturally to me. I view the universe as a myriad of problems to solve. I do not accept anything on face value without some skepticism. I will take something apart in order to discover what must be hidden there that will explain what it is or how it works. When I have a problem to solve, I look for many similar examples. I compare the examples, looking for distinctions and for what is missing. I determine or design a structure that will help me analyze the problem. I systematically initiate changes and run tests one by one until I solve the problem. I have a high tolerance for ambiguity and uncertainty, so I can easily consider many alternatives and think conditionally (if…, then…) in a search for solutions. Problems often need to be completely rethought or redesigned with different assumptions to make them solvable.

Ideas are independent entities. They are meant to be challenged, modified, and redefined. I may have a great amount of conviction about an idea and speak in such a way that others believe I am certain it is the truth, yet I am quick to discard the idea if it is proven false. Of course, this proof requires a solid, logically consistent argument. I can discuss, critique, analyze, and hypothesize about any idea or theory, but I am most satisfied when the topic is within an area of my expertise. I expect others to challenge my ideas, but I can be offended when others don't acknowledge the logical process by which my ideas were formed.

I prefer to direct my own life, living according to my own standards. I often pay only secondary attention to the customary and conventional, except in important situations. Relationships must fit into a particular structure in the larger scheme of things. I am usually drawn to people who share a common interest in an area of my expertise. I interact with them for intellectual stimulation and to test my ideas. I have a tendency to treat people as just another variable to consider.

WHAT I NEED FROM OTHERS

Allow me to think for myself and give me room to be creative. I want to be taken seriously. Don't rush me if you want quality. Work with me to meet long-term goals, even if they don't seem to pay off immediately.

HOW OTHERS PERCEIVE ME

Generally I am perceived as intelligent. Others may also view me as lacking emotion, or they may misinterpret what emotion I do show. They often view me as having particular talents rather than seeing my talents as intrinsic to who I am.

Essential Qualities of the Rational Temperament
NEEDS AND VALUES

The Rational's core needs are for mastery of concepts, knowledge, and competence. Rationals want to understand the operating principles of the universe and to learn or even develop theories for everything. They value expertise, logical consistency, concepts, and ideas, and they seek progress. Rationals tend toward pragmatic, utilitarian actions with a technology focus. They trust logic above all else. They tend to be skeptical and they highly value precision in language. Their learning style is conceptual, and Rationals want to know the underlying principles that generate the details and facts, rather than the details alone.

TALENTS

Rationals prefer using their gifts of strategic analysis to approach all situations. They constantly examine the relationship of the means to the overall vision and goal. No strangers to complexity, theories, and models, they like to think of all possible contingencies and develop multiple plans for handling them. They abstractly analyze a situation and consider previously unthought-of possibilities. Research, analysis, searching for patterns, and developing hypotheses are quite likely to be their natural modi operandi.

The Idealist Temperament

For Idealists, life is a process of cultivating relationships, pursuing self-actualization, and developing the potentials of those around them.

Born with a predisposition for the abstract, global, and personal, Idealists tend to focus on human potential, ethics, culture, quality of life, metaphysics, and personal growth. With such a focus, they often excel at communication, especially metaphor and imaginative narrative. Relating to others empathically, they have a keen ability to reflect and anticipate unspoken issues and intentions of others. They likewise excel at giving "strokes," interacting enthusiastically, personalizing the impersonal, sharing in participatory leadership, and empowering and facilitating growth in those with whom they come in contact. Thus they appear to be natural catalysts of group formations and interaction.

They place a high value on authenticity and integrity in people, relationships, and organizations. They engage in activities because they are meaningful, rather than because they are routine, mandatory, efficient, or entertaining. The power orientation of Idealists expresses itself in a search for fame, recognition, or personal impact upon society.

They are apt to exude warmth and a general mood of enthusiasm. They seek affiliation, harmony, and cooperation in social situations and often adopt a nurturing role toward those with whom they come in contact. Believing in the fundamental goodness of humankind, they maintain a generally optimistic, credulous, receptive, and accepting point of view toward the world.

Idealists come into a situation with an immediate impression of what's going on within and between the people. They take in the experience of the group and receive insights into the dynamics at work long before others do and usually beyond what others perceive. These insights are often vague impressions, although some will be quite powerful. Exploring relationships in all their forms is part of the human experience for them. They can call things as they see them or intervene in a creative way, acting as catalysts for growth. Ethical considerations and the impact on the web of relationships are part of empathizing with others. They enter, maintain, and leave relationships with their eyes wide open. Idealists cannot help but explore their feelings and how they feel about those feelings—feelings mean values. Idealists operate out of their values and intuitive perceptions and are often surprised when others lack awareness of the deep issues below the surface, from the past and for the future. They usually have a sense of where a person will be in the future. Idealists may show a different side in work environments, setting boundaries with an awareness of what they can afford to care about. They constantly balance seemingly contradictory needs for unity and empathy with others with their need for their own unique identity.

They most admire people of great integrity and commitment, the messiahs and sages of the world, and shun or despise the wishy-washy, the mundane, and the fake. They are stressed by the impersonal and the impervious and can suffer sometimes excruciating alienation in situations where their needs for relationship, significance, and esteem are not met. A divisive, argumentative, competitive atmosphere offends them and brings out their desire to rescue any victims or leave the scene. They can be troubled by a loss of their ability to experience or express unconditional positive regard. They do their best in environments that convey such positive regard, recognize their uniqueness, and provide validation, interaction, receptivity, and support.

They are a culture's foremost humanists and focus primarily on the meanings of humanity's past and the possibilities for its future.

Self-Portrait of the Idealist Temperament
As an Idealist...

I believe people and relationships are the most important aspects of my life. I am naturally empathic. When I interact with people, it is important for me to step inside their skin and see out through their eyes. This gives me confidence in how I can best help that person grow. I believe we are meant to lead meaningful and purposeful lives, and I like to act as a catalyst for helping other people identify their life purpose and what is meaningful to them. It is easy for me to inspire, appreciate, and reveal the best in others. I am a good listener and a good friend or mentor.

I view all individuals as having a unique identity with special gifts to contribute to the universe. It is important that every person be nurtured for who they are, not what others want of them. I will defend the right of anyone to do what he or she believes as long as no one else comes to harm, and likewise I will act in accordance with my own beliefs.

I respect myself and others when they are authentic. I respect people who show their true selves and do not wear false fronts. It is easy for me to see the deep motivation and inner workings behind what people do and say. So when a person says or does something incongruent with what I see, it is difficult for me to believe the person. Occasionally I mistake what I see inside the person, but usually my insight is correct. Often others are not even aware of their own incongruity, and that is when I go to work. I provide emotional support and listen to their life stories. I have a talent for subtly drawing people out. In the process they gain insight into their own beliefs, gifts, meaning, and purpose. Sometimes I want people to grow when they don't want to or are not ready. It is physically painful for me to see potential in another person who is not able or willing to actualize that potential. Maturity and practice help me know when it is appropriate to push someone and when it is not.

I envision an ideal world where every individual is self-actualized, contributing his or her gifts and reaping satisfaction, and where we all live in harmonious community. In support of this, I am often dedicated to causes that will bring about change to the quality of life in a deep way. I utilize my natural talents as a counselor and diplomat to bring together different perspectives. I have a gift for communicating complex images of purpose and vision through metaphor, which allows each person to visualize his or her own meaning and contribution.

I am particularly aware of the ethical merits of actions and beliefs. Because it is so easy for me to imagine how words and actions will affect people, I am constantly on guard to ensure that people will not be negatively affected. I will go to great lengths to thwart what I believe to be unethical behavior, and it is very difficult for people who have behaved unethically to regain my trust and respect.

Passion, romance, images, dreams, beliefs, intuition, and ideals are all dimensions of what it is to be me. At times I am disappointed that individuals, groups, communities, and situations don't live up to my idealized expectations. I like to hope that somehow they can live up to those expectations. I always have some hope, even in the darkest moments, that if we all learn from each other and work together, we can overcome our shortcomings and attain the ideal. We are a unified whole, ever interconnected. What happens to others, happens to me.

WHAT I NEED FROM OTHERS

A personal connection is imperative for me. I must feel that each person is acting authentically, and I must feel that people will accept me if I act authentically. I expect open discourse and personal sharing. I want to tell my stories as well as listen to others' stories. I need some feedback assuring me that people believe in me and my life purpose. I look for a willingness to stand together in the face of conflict and misunderstanding with the belief that working through the issues will only strengthen our bond.

HOW OTHERS PERCEIVE ME

Other people view me as a people person, someone who demonstrates empathy easily and makes others feel good about who they are. They commend my communication skills and say I am a natural teacher, counselor, and mentor. They also believe I wish for too much, and they are afraid they may not be able to live up to the ideal image I have of them. They may describe me as imaginative, idealistic, mysterious, intuitive, gullible, friendly, empowering, committed, and genuine.

Essential Qualities of the Idealist Temperament
NEEDS AND VALUES

The Idealist's core needs are for the meaning and significance that come from having a sense of purpose and working toward some greater good. Idealists need to have a sense of unique identity. They value unity, self-actualization, and authenticity. Idealists prefer cooperative interactions with a focus on ethics and morality. They tend to trust their intuitions and impressions first and then seek to find the logic and the data to support them. Given their need for empathic relationships, they learn more easily when they can relate to the instructor and the group.

TALENTS

Idealists tend to be gifted at unifying diverse people and helping individuals realize their potential. They build bridges between people through empathy and the clarification of deeper issues. They use these same skills to help people work through difficulties. Thus, Idealists can make excellent mediators, helping people and companies solve conflicts through mutual cooperation. If working on a global level, Idealists will be championing a cause. If working on an individual level, they focus on the growth and development of the person.

The I in TEAM

	ARTISAN	GUARDIAN
Core Needs	• Freedom to act on needs of the moment • To have impact	• Membership, belonging, a place • Responsibility
Some Core Values	• Variety • Skillful performance	• Security • Predictability
Talents	• Tactics • Performance	• Logistics • Protection
Language	• Colorful	• Factual
Communication Tools	• Anecdotes • Questions	• Comparisons • Measurements
Best Environments	• Stimulating • Varied	• Organized • Secure
Stressors	• Constraint • Boredom • Lack of impact	• Abandonment • Insubordination • Lack of belonging
Leadership Methods	• Taking action	• Giving cautions
Preferred Feedback	• Immediate	• Corrective

FINDING A BEST-FIT TEMPERAMENT

	RATIONAL	IDEALIST
Core Needs	• Knowledge and competence • Mastery	• Deep meaning and significance • Unique identity
Some Core Values	• Progress • Logical consistency	• Authenticity • Empathic relationships
Talents	• Strategy • Design	• Diplomacy • Advocacy
Language	• Scholarly	• Dramatic
Communication Tools	• Conditions • Precise definitions	• Metaphors • Universals
Best Environments	• Innovative • Intellectual	• Expressive • Personal
Stressors	• Powerlessness • Incompetence • Lack of knowledge	• Insincerity • Betrayal • Lack of integrity
Leadership Methods	• Developing strategies	• Giving praise
Preferred Feedback	• Expert	• Highly personalized

CLARIFYING YOUR TEMPERAMENT

5

By this point, you may see yourself in some of these patterns. Perhaps you are very clear about which pattern fits you the best. Most often, however, people find themselves in multiple patterns. That is understandable because the patterns are characteristic of abstract categories, and real people are complex living systems with many aspects to them.

Everyone has access to the needs, values, and talents of all four temperaments, but one temperament is a "best fit." One set of core needs, values, and talents is what drives us more than others. For some people, this best fit says it all. For others, there seems to be a hierarchy of needs at play, and a description of these people as having only one temperament would be incomplete. These people often claim a secondary or even a tertiary temperament.

This self-discovery process is like shopping for shoes. You want to find the best fit, one that supports you and doesn't cramp you. Use the following pages to help you sort out your own particular hierarchy and find which temperament pattern is really yours. Experience has shown that once people find their true temperament pattern, they experience a rush of energy and delight in knowing who they are. From that time forward, they can take charge of their lives and make better choices to have their needs met. They can also more easily manage their stress and attract the resources and opportunities they need.

Based on your look at the patterns so far, where do you fit? Which one is the least like you? Rate it a number four. Then ask yourself, If I had to give up or do without one of the remaining three, which one would that be? Rate it a number three. Use the following five pages to help you sort out which one of the two remaining temperament patterns is your best-fit temperament.

Things-in-Common

We often relate to more than one temperament pattern because each pattern has something in common with the others. These things-in-common reveal themselves in the interactions between people, especially in our communications. As you try to sort out which temperament is the best fit for you, you may identify a preference for one or another of the following dynamics, which are at play when the temperaments interact. These dynamics are:

- Abstract versus concrete language—The way we tend to think about things and the way we use words
- Affiliative versus pragmatic roles—The way we prefer to interact with others
- Structure versus motive focus—Where we focus our attention when interacting

These dynamics are always operating when we interact with others, and if we become polarized along these dimensions, communication can become extremely difficult. However, we need to remember that we have at least one thing in common with every temperament. Exploring these dynamics may help you further clarify which temperament is your best fit.

Language: Ways to Use Words

Language provides us with a way to think about things, a way to translate back and forth between our thoughts, feelings, and world-views and the events and people in our world. Our language usually reflects our natural way of viewing the world. Language can be classified as two kinds—abstract and concrete.

ABSTRACT LANGUAGE

Abstract language describes abstractions, concepts, and patterns referencing only as much sensory detail as needed. This is the language of implications, hypotheses, or symbolic meanings. It references what is theoretical, not applied or practical. There is usually little reference to specific situations, instances, or experiences. Abstract language is the language of choice to describe what exists mainly in the mind and in an envisioned, ideal world. This language describes a reality that is not easily seen but is just as real as the tangible world.

Those with a preference for the Idealist temperament often use global and impressionistic abstract language so people listening can make their own meanings and find their own identities. In the Rational temperament pattern, abstract language is usually more precise and specific with the goal of increased clarity leading to knowledge.

CONCRETE LANGUAGE

Concrete language describes tangible realities backed up by sensory observations. The goal of concrete language is to make things more "real" or specific. It describes what exists, existed, or will exist in reality and what is perceptible to the senses. It can stand for an object as it exists in nature, not the abstracted attributes of that object. It relates to material objects by reviewing events, facts, images, memories, and how things look, feel, taste, and sound.

For those with a preference for the Guardian temperament, concrete language often references past events, sequences of events, the linking of one fact to another, or physical responses to past events. In the Artisan temperament pattern, concrete language is used to heighten awareness of physical reality by vivid, sensory descriptions of immediate or near-future events or experiences, often in a random fashion, that create a tangible image in the mind of the listener.

Roles: Ways of Interacting

When people come together to accomplish something, they typically either refer to other people and strive to get the job done together in an affiliative manner, or refer to the desired outcome and more autonomously take whatever action they see fit to achieve the outcome in a pragmatic manner. These are the two major kinds of roles we take in our interactions—affiliative or pragmatic.

AFFILIATIVE ROLES

Affiliative roles require that people act in community, with a sense of what is good for the team. They may be people focused or task focused. They may be practical or idealistic. No matter what happens, affiliative roles always maintain some sense of cooperation and interdependence. In this way of interacting, it is important to have roles defined and to get agreement.

For those with a preference for the Guardian temperament, affiliative roles include clear lines of responsibility and authority. This orderliness makes it easy for people to know where they belong and how they fit in. The concern is to maintain the team. In the Idealist temperament pattern, affiliative roles help people know who they are—their unique identity—and provide a way to find meaning and purpose in what they do.

PRAGMATIC ROLES

Pragmatic roles require that individuals act in accordance with what they see must be done to get the desired result. They too may be people focused or task focused. They too may be practical or idealistic. When a decision must be made or an action must be taken, the first inclination is to act more independently regardless of norms or consensus. In this way of interacting, individual autonomy is very important.

For those with a preference for the Artisan temperament, pragmatic roles give the freedom and autonomy to act according to the needs of the moment. They enable seizing those opportunities that don't last. In the Rational temperament pattern, pragmatic roles ensure a focus on the overall strategy and vision of a project and give a sense of mastery and self-control.

Attention: Interest and Focus

We can focus our attention on different things. Often in our communications we find our interest and attention going to either the structure of a situation or to people's motives. Conflict can often result from people focusing on different aspects and thus promoting different actions. Guardians and Rationals tend to focus more on structure, and Idealists and Artisans tend to focus more on motives.

STRUCTURE

For those with a preference for the Guardian temperament pattern, the interest in structure is concrete and procedural. Guardian structures provide rules, norms, roles, and responsibilities. Examples include sequential outlines, family trees, and organizational charts. These structures serve to inform others about what is appropriate and what can be expected.

In the Rational temperament pattern, the structural attention goes to the abstract and multidimensional, as in logic and matrices, coordinates, and organizing principles. Rational structures provide implementation strategies, and at the same time they provide ways to catalogue and master the principles of how the world operates. The goal is for all to learn to be more competent and efficient within the system.

MOTIVE

For those with a preference for the Artisan temperament pattern, attention is paid first to what an individual "gets" out of a situation. Motives are the reasons people act; motives must be attended to in order to get the desired results. Knowing a person's motives provides the Artisan with cues to freely respond as that person pursues his or her wants and needs.

In the Idealist temperament pattern, attention goes to others' meanings and purposes. For Idealists, motives represent a person's spirit and higher purpose in life. Motives must be attended to because understanding them provides opportunities to achieve consensus and to work together toward a common goal and at the same time achieve a purpose.

Four Varieties of Each Temperament

The temperament theme plays out in four different ways. Reading snapshot descriptions of these different ways may help you find a more accurate fit.

Each of the four temperaments expresses in four different ways. Sometimes it helps you clarify your temperament if you can see some of the variations since some of the variations can make that temperament look like other temperaments.

On the eight pages beginning on page 68 are brief snapshots of the four varieties of each temperament. If you feel fairly confident of the fit of one temperament, you can confirm that fit by reading the four snapshots within that temperament. If one of these doesn't ring true for you, you may need to reconsider and try a second temperament. If you are sorting between two temperaments read the varieties of these two temperaments to see if that helps you find a fit.

If your are already certain of your temperament, then you can skip to section III: Integration of the Stages of Team Development and Temperament.

FOUR VARIETIES OF EACH TEMPERAMENT

Foreseer Developer (See page 74)	**Harmonizer Clarifier** (See page 75)	**Planner Inspector** (See page 70)	**Protector Supporter** (See page 71)
IDEALIST		**GUARDIAN**	
Envisioner Mentor (See page 74)	**Discoverer Advocate** (See page 75)	**Implementor Supervisor** (See page 70)	**Facilitator Caretaker** (See page 71)
Conceptualizer Director (See page 72)	**Designer Theorizer** (See page 73)	**Analyzer Operator** (See page 68)	**Composer Producer** (See page 69)
RATIONAL		**ARTISAN**	
Strategist Mobilizer (See page 72)	**Explorer Inventor** (See page 73)	**Promoter Executor** (See page 68)	**Motivator Presenter** (See page 69)

Four Varieties of the Artisan Temperament
CONCRETE LANGUAGE / PRAGMATIC ROLES / INTEREST IN MOTIVE

Analyzer Operator

Theme is action-driven problem solving. Talents lie in operating all kinds of tools and instruments and using frameworks for solving problems. Keen observers of the environment, they are a storehouse of data and facts relevant to analyzing and solving problems. Thrive on challenging situations and having the freedom to craft clever solutions and do whatever it takes to fix things and make them work. Take pride in their skill and virtuosity, which they seem to effortlessly acquire.

THIS SOUNDS LIKE ME ❏

Promoter Executor

Theme is promoting. Talents lie in persuading others and expediting to make things happen. Have an engaging, winning style that others are drawn to. Adept at picking up on minimal nonverbal cues. Anticipate the actions and reactions of others and thus win their confidence. Like the excitement and challenge of negotiating, selling, making deals, arbitrating, and in general, achieving the impossible. Thrive on action and the freedom to use all resources at hand to get desired outcomes.

THIS SOUNDS LIKE ME ❏

Composer Producer

Theme is composing, using whatever is at hand to get a harmonious, aesthetic result. Talents lie in combining, varying, and improvising, frequently in the arts but also in business and elsewhere. With their senses keenly tuned in they become totally absorbed in the action of the moment, finding just what fits the situation or the composition. Thrive on having the freedom to vary what they do until they get just the right effect. Take action to help others and demonstrate values. Kind, and sensitive to the suffering of others.

THIS SOUNDS LIKE ME ❏

Motivator Presenter

Theme is performance. Warm, charming, and witty. Want to impact and help others, to evoke their enjoyment, and to stimulate them to act. Want to make a difference and do something meaningful. Often masterful at showmanship, entertaining, motivating, and presenting. Thrive on social interaction, joyful living, and the challenge of the unknown. Like helping people get what they want and need, facilitating them to get results.

THIS SOUNDS LIKE ME ❏

Four Varieties of the Guardian Temperament
CONCRETE LANGUAGE / AFFILIATIVE ROLES / INTEREST IN STRUCTURE

Planner Inspector

Theme is planning and monitoring, ensuring predictable quality. Thorough, systematic, and careful. See discrepancies, omissions, and pitfalls. Talents lie in administrating and regulating. Dependable, realistic, and sensible. Want to conserve the resources of the organization, group, family, or culture and persevere toward that goal. Thrive on planning ahead and being prepared. Like helping others through their roles as parent, supervisor, teammate, and community volunteer.

THIS SOUNDS LIKE ME ❏

Implementor Supervisor

Theme is supervising, with an eye to the traditions and regulations of the group. Responsible, hardworking, and efficient. Interested in ensuring that standards are met, resources conserved, and consequences delivered. Talents lie in bringing order, structure, and completion. Want to keep order so the organization, group, family, or culture will be preserved. Thrive on organizing and following through with commitments and teaching others how to be successful.

THIS SOUNDS LIKE ME ❏

Protector Supporter

Theme is protecting and caretaking, making sure their charges are safe from harm. Talents lie in making sure everything is taken care of so others can succeed and accomplish their goals. Desiring to serve individual needs, often work long hours. Quietly friendly, respectful, unassuming. Thrive on serving quietly without fanfare. Devoted to doing whatever is necessary to ensure shelter and safety, warning about pitfalls and dangers, and supporting along the way.

THIS SOUNDS LIKE ME ❑

Facilitator Caretaker

Theme is providing, ensuring that physical needs are met. Talents lie in supporting others and supplying them with what they need. Genuinely concerned about the welfare of others, making sure they are comfortable and involved. Use their sociability to nurture established institutions. Warm, considerate, thoughtful, friendly. Want to please and maintain harmonious relationships. Thrive on helping others and bringing people together.

THIS SOUNDS LIKE ME ❑

Four Varieties of the Rational Temperament
ABSTRACT LANGUAGE / PRAGMATIC ROLES / INTEREST IN STRUCTURE

Conceptualizer Director

Theme is strategizing, envisioning, and masterminding. Talents lie in defining goals, creating detailed plans, and outlining contingencies. Devise strategy, give structure, establish complex plans to reach distant goals dictated by a strong vision of what is needed in the long run. Thrive on putting theories to work and are open to any and all ideas that can be integrated into the complex systems they seek to understand. Drive themselves hard to master what is needed to make progress toward goals.

THIS SOUNDS LIKE ME ❑

Strategist Mobilizer

Theme is directing and mobilizing. Talents lie in developing policy, establishing plans, coordinating and sequencing events, and implementing strategy. Excel at directing others in reaching the goals dictated by their strong vision of the organization. Thrive on marshaling forces to get plans into action. Natural organization builders and almost always find themselves taking charge in ineffective situations. They enjoy creating efficiently structured systems and setting priorities to achieve goals.

THIS SOUNDS LIKE ME ❑

Designer Theorizer

Theme is designing and configuring. Talents lie in grasping the underlying principles of something and defining its essential qualities. Seek to define precisely and bring coherence to systems based on the pattern of organization that is naturally there. Easily notice inconsistencies. Enjoy elegant theories and models for their own sake and for use in solving technical and human problems. Interested in theorizing, analyzing, and learning. Thrive on exploring, understanding, and explaining how the world works.

THIS SOUNDS LIKE ME ❑

Explorer Inventor

Theme is inventing, finding ingenious solutions to people problems and technical problems. Talents lie in developing ideas into functional and innovative applications that are the first of their kind. Thrive on finding new ways to use theories to make systems more efficient and people better off. Hunger for new projects. Have faith in their ability to instantly come up with new approaches that will work. Engineers of human relationships and systems as well as in the more scientific and technological domains.

THIS SOUNDS LIKE ME ❑

Four Varieties of the Idealist Temperament
ABSTRACT LANGUAGE / AFFILIATIVE ROLES / INTEREST IN MOTIVE

Foreseer Developer

Theme is foresight. Use their insights to deal with complexity in issues and people, often with a strong sense of "knowing" before others know themselves. Talents lie in developing and guiding people. Trust their inspirations and visions, using them to help others. Thrive on helping others resolve deep personal and ethical dilemmas. Private and complex, they bring a quiet enthusiasm and industry to projects that are part of their vision.

THIS SOUNDS LIKE ME ❑

Envisioner Mentor

Theme is mentoring, leading people to achieve their potential and become more of who they are. Talents lie in empathizing with profound interpersonal insight and in influencing others to learn, grow, and develop. Lead using their exceptional communication skills, enthusiasm, and warmth to gain cooperation toward meeting the ideals they hold for the individual or the organization. Catalysts who draw out the best in others. Thrive on empathic connections. Frequently called on to help others with personal problems.

THIS SOUNDS LIKE ME ❑

Harmonizer Clarifier

Theme is advocacy and integrity. Talents lie in helping people clarify issues, values, and identity. Support anything that allows the unfolding of the person. Encourage growth and development with quiet enthusiasm. Loyal advocates and champions, caring deeply about their causes and a few special people. Interested in contemplating life's mysteries, virtues, and vices in their search for wholeness. Thrive on healing conflicts, within and between, and taking people to the center of themselves.

THIS SOUNDS LIKE ME ❏

Discoverer Advocate

Theme is inspiration, both of themselves and others. Talents lie in grasping profound significance, revealing truths, and motivating others. Very perceptive of others' hidden motives and purposes. Interested in everything about individuals and their stories as long as they are genuine. Contagious enthusiasm for "causes" that further good and develop latent potential and the same zeal for disclosing dishonesty and inauthenticity. Frequently moved to enthusiastically communicate their "message."

THIS SOUNDS LIKE ME ❏

Moving On

Now that you have a sense of the four temperaments, read on to see how temperament differences play out on remote as well as co-located teams. Seeing how the temperaments differ in each stage of team development will not only help you understand yourself better, but also give you a way to interact more productively with team members.

INTEGRATION
OF THE
STAGES OF
TEAM
DEVELOPMENT
AND
TEMPERAMENT

FORMING

6

Understanding Temperament and the Forming Stage

The Forming stage is a critical stage in the process of team development. For your currently forming team, which of the following characteristics are true?

STAGE 1: FORMING CHARACTERISTICS	TRUE FOR MY TEAM
Some excitement, anticipation, and optimism	
Some anxiety: Where do I fit?	
Expectation: Looking to the leader for guidance and direction	
Politeness among team members	
A cautious atmosphere	
Need in individuals to find a place and establish themselves	

The following questions, which we identified in chapter 2, are being asked during the Forming stage:

- What's our purpose?
- What will my role be?
- Who are these other people?
- How will we work together?

Questions (Back-of-mind concerns)

In addition to having the preceding questions answered, to become really engaged in the team, team members also need to feel that their core needs will be met. Even though concerns about their core needs are likely to be outside their awareness, these concerns will influence their behaviors. These "back-of-mind" concerns are being asked (often unconsciously) by people of all four temperaments.

IDEALIST	GUARDIAN
• Do I care about our work? • Do I have a meaningful role in this team? • Can I relate to these people?	• What will I be responsible for? • Do I have a place in this team? • Will these team members do their part?
RATIONAL	ARTISAN
• Is there room for my area of expertise? • Do I have the competence required? • Are these people competent?	• Is there room in this team for me to make an impact? • Will I have the freedom to act as I see fit? • What's in it for everyone to be on this team?

Remote Team Concerns

When a remote team is just forming, the questions in people's minds are the same as for co-located teams. The challenge, though, is that there is often not a forum in which to get answers to the questions.

It is rare that a remote team can come together for a face-to-face meeting to get the team started, so this stage is often extended while people try to figure out the answers to their questions.

Many co-located teams skip this stage, even though for them it is easier than it is for remote teams. It's very easy, then, for a remote team to jump into work without any focus on helping team members through this stage.

Buy-In Questions

While the team as a whole needs to define "why we are here" and "who we are," individuals will be looking for more specific answers based on their temperament. Providing for these needs supplies the "buy-in" needed by people of different temperaments.

IDEALIST	GUARDIAN
• Are people well intentioned? Will people cooperate? • Is there a sense of good will?	• Do we have the people and tools we need to be successful? • Will we be a team long enough to make it worthwhile?
RATIONAL	ARTISAN
• How does what we're doing fit into the scheme of things? • Is this well-thought-out?	• Is there anything for me to do here? • Is this going to be a waste of time or boring?

Needs from Leader

It's early in the life of the team and some of the members are looking to the team leader to provide the guidance and structure needed to get started. In order to satisfy all members, the team leader must make sure the following tasks are accomplished for each temperament.

IDEALIST	GUARDIAN
• Take time to get to know each other. • Define a purpose that has meaning. • Recognize and affirm unique talents.	• Clarify roles. • Define a structure for forming the team. • Provide time frames.
RATIONAL	ARTISAN
• Share members' knowledge and expertise. • Define the goal. • Give a rationale for any pre-scribed processes.	• Provide opportunity for skillful performance and freedom of action. • Get started quickly. • Set boundaries and parameters early.

Proactively providing for these needs can move a team forward more quickly into the Storming stage where differences will begin to appear. Dealing with the differences can accelerate the team's process in a productive way.

Remote Team Concerns

If there is no start-up face-to-face meeting, structure considerations are often assumed and relationship issues are ignored. Without a conversation, people will tend to work independently to figure out what they need or to make it happen.

This independent movement could result in a variety of outcomes, including the following:

- A lengthening of the time it takes to do the task or project
- Work "falling through the cracks"
- Duplicate or unnecessary work being done
- Paralysis in waiting for clarity about team structure and relationships

If these needs from the leader aren't met, the Storming stage will often be more turbulent and longer than necessary, and it might be more difficult for the team to progress to the next stage of development.

Actions and Tools to Maximize the Forming Stage

To make the most of the Forming stage, hold a meeting or a series of meetings as soon as the team is formed. These meetings, while best face to face, can be conducted with teleconference calls, e-meetings, video conferences, or other technology.

In this meeting or meetings, the following accomplishments are important:

1. Clarify purpose
2. Build relationships
3. Dialogue about differences
4. Define goals and objectives
5. Clarify roles and identify skills
6. Clarify boundaries
7. Establish team norms or operating guidelines
8. Identify tasks to begin right away

Some of these items relate more to the task dimension (T) of teamwork, some to the relationship dimension (R), and one relates to both. Be careful not to focus only on task or only on relationship actions.

"T" 1. Clarify Purpose

The team needs the answer to the questions, "Why have we been put together?" and "What are we supposed to accomplish?" These answers are likely to come from the organization or the team leader. If they don't, then the leader needs to guide a discussion to clarify the team's purpose.

"R" 2. Build Relationships

We do things for people we know. For the team to accomplish work together, relationship building is key. Some relationship building will happen over the life of the team. Deliberate efforts to build relationships among all team members early on will pay off in moving the team to more productive levels of performance.

Team members need to get to know one another on many levels, including personality style, work background, and personal interests. Good meeting openers or coffee conversations to facilitate relationship building include the following:

- What did you do this weekend?
- What's your favorite leisure pastime?
- What are you proud of?
- What are your goals and objectives this week?
- What are your key challenges this week?

Even when you can't meet face to face to do relationship building, you can use technology to work on it. On Web sites or team databases, you can include photos and personal information. On conference calls or e-meetings, remember to use the above meeting openers to learn more about one another.

One team we know had a place in its team database called the "water cooler," where members posted personal information such as family photographs, news of births, vacation plans, and so on. Team members could read the team news when they had time, and it helped everyone feel more connected with each other.

"R" 3. Dialogue about Differences

It is also helpful to learn about personality differences. Temperament is a good place to start. As individuals understand how they are different and alike, they can be more open to ways of working successfully together. Bringing these differences to the surface early prevents wasteful conflict over what can become the strength of a team—differences. So start with temperament and move on to other differences you are aware of.

"T" 4. Define Goals and Objectives

What is the work of this team? How will the team measure success and what are the milestones? Team members are likely to have very different views of the goals. Temperament differences contribute to seeing things differently, so be sure to include everyone in clarifying the goals. Some people are less inclined than others to set measurements and look for milestones. Some will want to spend more time on this. Find a good balance to be sure this action is taken.

"T" 5. Clarify Roles and Identify Skills

Who brings what talents and skills to the team and how will those talents and skills be used? The tool on page 172–173 can be useful for exploring temperament talents. The team will also want to understand other skills, knowledge, and experiences that each member has. Looking at skills and talents is often just a starting point and will need to be pursued further in the Storming stage.

"T" 6. Clarify Boundaries

What does this team have authority to decide and what must it get permission for? If it appears that a boundary will impact the team's ability to accomplish its work, that boundary should be challenged. When a team challenges a boundary, it should know who owns the boundary and put together a case for changing it.

Example: A team has a boundary stipulating that it may not spend more than $250 on technology without permission from the finance department. Many of the items the team needs to successfully implement its project fall in the range of $200 to $450 and often take two days to receive after being ordered. Currently the spending-approval process takes one week, causing the team to lose time after members decide what product they need.

The team should put together a case for extending the boundary to $500 and present it to the appropriate person in the finance department.

In the remote environment, getting permission can add significantly to the turnaround time on work. Time spent early in the life of the team clarifying boundaries can positively impact the team's ability to accomplish work productively down the road.

"T" and "R" 7. Establish Team Norms or Operating Guidelines

Establishing norms or operating guidelines is important for teams, particularly remote teams. Some common norms are
- How often do we meet?
- How do we make decisions?
- How do we treat each other?

It is important to set time for each team member to share how he or she likes to receive feedback and handle conflict, and to address other relationship and communication issues that can come up. Then the team can agree on some ground rules for interacting with each other under pressure.

Remote teams also need to establish norms around technology and connections. For example,

- Which tools will be used when? "T"
    - Conference calls
    - Shared databases
    - E-meetings
    - Instant messaging
    - E-mail

- How quickly will we respond to requests? "R"
  Since we can't see each other, we need to know what our commitments are to each other. The response times may be different on e-mail, databases, and voice mail.

- What is each person's preferred way to be contacted? "R"
    - Should I call your cell phone or your business phone first?
    - Do you prefer to receive e-mail or voice mail?
    - How should I contact you when it's urgent?
    - What are your guidelines for your cell phone after hours?
    - What hours do you have your cell phone turned on?

"T" 8. Identify Tasks to Begin Right Away

With the team knowledge that's been collected, it should be relatively easy to determine the tasks to be done, who should do them, and the priority of each task. Be sure you take time to specify these things rather than assume people will know what to do.

If these eight actions are taken, team members of each temperament will feel included and feel they have a place on the team.

Of the eight actions, which are most important to you?
1. Clarify Purpose
2. Build Relationships
3. Dialogue about Differences
4. Define Goals and Objectives
5. Clarify Roles and Identify Skills
6. Clarify Boundaries
7. Establish Team Norms or Operating Guidelines
8. Identify Tasks to Begin Right Away

For your currently forming team, which actions have been done?

Which actions need to be taken?

What are your hopes and fears for this team?
Hopes:

Fears:

How do these relate to your temperament?

Moving On to the Storming Stage

For some team members the Forming stage is a comfortable place. Spending time getting to know each other and laying out the goals, milestones, norms, and so on can be satisfying and feel safe. However, the team needs to do real work and must move beyond the comfort of getting organized and connected.

But don't move before you are ready.

Example: A software development team (one Artisan, one Idealist, and two Rationals) was working on a complex project with many almost-unsolvable problems. Nobody was enjoying the work and there was underlying tension between team members. Conflict emerged about how to get the work done and how to better use the talents on the team.

As a solution, the team went back to the Forming stage and determined that it didn't have a clear and common picture of what it was being asked to do. The process to identify the problem moved fairly quickly because the team had already done some good work around relationship building and sharing of expertise when it first formed.

While this team had done most of the forming, it needed to revisit clarifying its purpose and boundaries. Given the preferences for abstract language on the part of three of the four team members, it was natural for them to not get enough detail about the purpose of the team in the beginning. Had the team members done this more concretely to start with, they probably wouldn't have had to revisit the task.

The realities of the work setting often require quickly moving on to do work. The guidelines presented in this chapter can help identify what Forming processes need to be revisited when early Storming happens.

STORMING

Understanding Temperament and the Storming Stage

As a team moves into the Storming stage of development, differences start to be noticed. Differences can be and often are interpreted as conflicting goals. The conflict can be very visible—arguments, flaming e-mail, and so on. Often, however, particularly in the remote workplace, the conflict is much less visible.

What words come to mind when you think of "conflict"? Our experience when we ask this question in a workshop is that well over half (often most) of the words that people share with us have negative connotations. The list usually includes words like "fight," "argue," "anger," "lose," and "confrontation."

Fortunately, we also hear some positive words when we ask these questions. We hear words such as "new ideas," "collaboration," "win-win," and "solutions."

While conflict often evokes a sense that something is wrong or bad, conflict can in fact serve a positive purpose for a team. If there were no conflicts in our lives, how boring would it be? If we all always agreed on everything, our solutions wouldn't likely be very creative.

Conflict is necessary for high performance. How conflict is viewed and managed in the team determines whether it ends up being positive and helping the team move toward high performance or negative and detracting from performance. Teams need to learn how to work through the conflict rather than allow the conflict to control them. They need to use their differences to enhance team outcomes.

For your currently storming team, which of the following characteristics are true?

Characteristic	True for My Team
Discrepancy between hopes and reality	
Disagreement about goals, tasks, and action plans	
Lack of progress toward goals	
Feelings of incompetence and confusion	
Competition for power and attention	
Formation of subgroups	
Scapegoating	
Resistance to being led	
Miscommunication	
Unresolved conflicts	

Remote Team Concerns

When conflict goes undetected or isn't dealt with, it often gets worse. Remote teams find several reasons for not dealing with conflict. When team members interact remotely, body language is missing, so it is difficult to assess how another person is reacting to a situation and easier to let it go than to engage and risk misreading the situation. Speaking on the telephone versus in person also puts a time pressure on the calling parties, so conflict is often left out of the discussion. And if the conflict seems to be temperament related, people may be hesitant to bring up the problem since they can't tell if others sense the same problem. Because of these issues, we have found that in remote teams, by the time conflict is identified it has often escalated into a much bigger issue than it was originally.

Blaming

The Storming stage is a place to work out the team's conflicts so that differences lead to performance. Everyone may have a different way of describing what isn't working in the team. In the Forming stage, we have questions and concerns. In the Storming stage, we often blame. When we blame we tend to think of "if only" solutions (if only we would…). Bringing up your "if only" solutions doesn't usually fix the problem. And since each temperament will have different "if onlys," other team members may not relate to your "if onlys."

IDEALIST	GUARDIAN
• We're not being honest with each other. • If only we'd deal with what is really important.	• There's no accountability in this team. • If only we could count on people to do what they are supposed to.
RATIONAL	ARTISAN
• We're not thinking things through logically. • If only we would discuss alternatives and become more efficient.	• We talk about doing things and nothing happens. • If only we'd just try some different things.

Triggers

Different aspects of a team's work may trigger the team into a downward spiral of blame and may increase the storming. These aspects will be different for different people based on whether their core needs are being met or are threatened. For each temperament the threat may begin as a sense of unease and then, when unresolved, may be experienced in the following ways.

IDEALIST	GUARDIAN
• Feeling hurt when not appreciated for unique personal contributions • Feeling apathetic when seeing no meaning or significance	• Feeling burdened by not understanding personal responsibilities • Feeling useless with no sense of place
RATIONAL	**ARTISAN**
• Feeling stupid in not knowing enough or not being competent enough • Feeling powerless with no sense of mastery or self-control	• Feeling trapped or stuck with no freedom to act • Feeling impotent with no ability to make an impact

In remote teams, when individuals have not had a chance to get to know each other, blame and storming may be triggered sooner than in a co-located team. When relationships have been built, people generally feel safer to check out these feelings.

Identifying the Conflicts

Identifying a conflict makes the conflict easier to diffuse and resolve. It can also help prevent unproductive conflict.

Blaming and its triggers are signs of conflict. Temperament differences can tell us what's behind those responses; various aspects of our temperament differences become sources of conflict:

- Mismatch of Talents and Roles
- Collision of Approaches
- Core Values
- Time Orientation
- Evaluating Solutions
- Styles of Learning
- Approach to Task and Relationships
- Polarities
    - Language Polarity
    - Role Assumption
    - Interest and Focus

Each of these conflict sources is dealt with in this chapter.

Mismatch of Talents and Roles

Team conflict can be caused by a mismatch between talents and roles/responsibilities. People whose talents do not match the responsibilities given to them in the team feel unappreciated. It's an individual issue that becomes a team issue because our performance suffers when we are doing tasks or projects that we don't like or don't have talent for.

People say or think, "I don't get to do what I do easily. It's a problem for me if there is no need for my talent on this team." There may be a need for that talent on the team, but team members may not be recognizing it or appreciating it.

Artisan Tactical Skill Set	Artisan "I never get to..."
• Read the current context, read the situation, and skillfully manage the situation.	• Solve problems.
• Effect a desired result, often coming up with a variety of solutions.	• Troubleshoot.
• Take action according to the needs of the moment, and plan the next move.	• Take immediate action.
• Cleverly display, compose, and perform with attention to impact and effect.	• Do it.
• Compose and produce just the right result that expresses the input of all those concerned.	• Vary what I do.
• Analyze and look at all the angles, getting a sense of the situation and then being free to operate in the moment as things change.	• Vary how I do it.
• Motivate others, often through a lively and moving presentation.	• Focus on the impact.
• Promote and execute actions in response to the varying demands of the situation, moving around obstacles when necessary.	• Show my stuff.
	• Do my thing.
	• Pull it off.

ARE YOUR TALENTS BEING USED IN THIS TEAM?

Guardian Logistical Skill Set	Guardian "I never get to..."
• Provide the logistical support and protection necessary for people to get things done right and to make sure things go well and don't go wrong.	• See it through to completion.
	• Set up logistical systems.
	• Share the history.
• Provide service and caretaking that help people get underway with the projects.	• Bring in enough data.
	• Keep things order.
• Get the right supplies and the right information the right place, at the right time, in the right quantity, the right quality, to the right people and not to the wrong people.	• Maintain traditions.
	• Point out where things could go wrong.
	• Conserve resources.
• Attend to people's comforts and make things easy for them.	• Make things useful.
	• Do what I'm supposed to do.
• Standardize, establish, and oversee policies and procedures that provide stability for the team.	
• Investigate what has happened before, carefully describe where the team wants to go and how to get there, and monitor the plan along the way.	
• Shelter and protect to ensure safety and well-being.	
• Examine, assess, and instruct to instruct to meet standards.	

ARE YOUR TALENTS BEING USED IN THIS TEAM?

Rational Strategic Skill Set	Rational "I never get to..."
• Think of and explain all the possible contingencies and influencing factors, and then design processes for achieving the objectives.	• Do a strategic analysis.
	• Look at contingencies.
	• Lay out a strategy.
• Abstractly analyze a situation and consider possibilities not previously thought of.	• Look at situations or problems in their full complexity.
• Look at the relationships between the goals and the means.	• Really define anything.
	• Think things through.
• Identify the ways and means to achieve a well-defined goal.	• Explore new possibilities.
	• Develop new models.
• Integrate ideas into cohesive theories and design processes that strategically meet the wants and needs of others.	• Create any new knowledge.
	• Show what I know.
• Implement a vision of the future, conceiving of a way to operate in the future as well as the steps needed to get there.	
• Generate and share a multitude of ideas and possibilities for action.	
• Mobilize and coordinate actions by others to implement a strategy.	

ARE YOUR TALENTS BEING USED IN THIS TEAM?

Idealist Diplomatic Skill Set	Idealist "I never get to..."
• Build bridges between people. • Have empathy. • Unify people by understanding and resolving deep issues while honoring individual uniqueness. • Move to a level of abstraction to see how two seemingly different views are alike and then choose a symbolic way of communicating the similarity. • Help others harmonize and clarify their values to bring unity to the team. • Have foresight and vision for developing the people involved, then communicate that vision in a way that is accepted and followed. • Help others find their path and inspire them to follow it. • Envision others meeting their potential and then mentor them to achieve the envisioned potential.	• Clarify the vision and values of the team. • Draw out the best in others. • Facilitate growth. • Mediate differences. • Work through difficulties. • Share insights and explore possibilities. • Explore deeper issues. • Help people cooperate. • Champion a cause. • Inspire others.

ARE YOUR TALENTS BEING USED IN THIS TEAM?

Example: A team of three management training professionals (a Guardian, an Artisan, and an Idealist) was in turmoil and
the members were dissatisfied with each other in different ways.
When the team set up workshops at a conference center, the
Artisan spent time chatting with the conference center staff,
and the Guardian spent time organizing the room and workshop
materials. The Guardian felt that the team should be setting up
the classroom. She did not appreciate the tactical networking the
Artisan did until later, when she saw that it helped the session go
smoothly. The Artisan was bristling at too much order and constraint that he felt was imposed by the Guardian. He thought the
Guardian should lighten up and have some fun. The Idealist spent
her time making peace with each of the others, one-on-one, so
that each thought the Idealist was on his or her side.

Each team member used his or her talents but didn't appreciate the others'. And the Idealist didn't use her diplomatic talents
for the good of the overall team but rather to maintain individual
relationships, so her efforts didn't serve to resolve the problem.
Ultimately, the three team members got some help from an outside coach and learned to appreciate the value each brought to
the team.

Collision of Approaches

With people of each temperament preferring different skill
sets, it is common for conflict to emerge around the different
approaches that people take to issues, discussions, and so on.
Each skill set has the potential for a unique collision with every
other skill set and for a way out of the collision. Each temperament pattern includes the following skill sets:

Artisan—Tactical
Guardian—Logistical
Rational—Strategic
Idealist —Diplomatic

The way out of the collisions is to focus on what the skill sets have in common to bridge the differences.

A COLLISION OF STRATEGY AND TACTICS

The way out of the strategy-tactics collision is to focus on the strength of both approaches in getting a larger goal met.

Strategy
Broader scope

Timing – Long future based on past and current influences

Tactics
Contextual scope

Timing – Now and next based on current realities

Example: A team of two Rationals and one Artisan was starting a project together and the members were discussing what work to do first: to complete specific work for a current client or to design the larger organizational deliverable that would impact all clients, current and future. The Rationals' argument was that what they do impacts the company's reputation with the client so it's important to look at the whole project before embarking on specific work. The Artisan's argument was that clients come first so it's important to meet the client's immediate need.

To resolve the clash between the strategic approach and the tactical approach, the team needed to have a discussion that demonstrated how both approaches were important and then to focus energy on how to meet both goals. There are several possible ways of helping each other see different views. Setting a time limit on the strategy discussion would have limited the Artisan's sense of wasting time and missing opportunities. Scheduling strategy time would have helped the Rationals feel that they weren't going to get sidetracked by firefighting.

A COLLISION OF STRATEGY AND LOGISTICS

The way out of the strategy-logistics collision is to focus on structure.

Strategy
Vision

Timing – Long future based on past and current influences

Logistics
Implementation

Timing – Near future based on lessons from the past

Example: Mary, a Guardian, has just joined a team. The leader has a preference for the Rational temperament. To bring Mary on board, he talks about his vision of the future. Mary just wants to know what she is supposed to do in order to support the team. They need to create a plan to show how Mary's responsibilities relate to the team's vision and to clarify her role in making the vision happen.

A COLLISION OF STRATEGY AND DIPLOMACY

The way out of the strategy-diplomacy collision is to find where the separate visions connect.

Strategy
Objective focus on goals and means

Focus on accuracy and truth

Diplomacy
Focus on implications for developing people

Focus on idealized and meaningful world

Example: Two members of a senior management team of a medium-size company find themselves disrupting the team with their conflict. One member (a Rational) brings all issues and decisions back to "bottom line" goals. The other member (an Idealist) connects all issues and decisions to the importance of people learning and growing as they work toward the organizational goals. They need to discuss the meaning behind their perspectives to agree on the importance of both perspectives in their decision making. Refocusing on organizational health and explaining the importance of financial health would help the Idealist connect to the vision of the Rational. Redefining growth and learning as ways to maximize the assets of the organization would help the Rational connect to the vision of the Idealist. Both visions connect to the greater good of organizational survival and health.

A COLLISION OF TACTICS AND LOGISTICS

The way out of the tactics-logistics collision is to focus on tangible outcomes.

Tactics
Adaptability

Timing – Now and
next based on current
realities

Logistics
Consistency

Timing – Near future
based on lessons from
the past

Example: The leader of a finance team (of eleven people) was frustrated by two members of the team who weren't getting along. Through some team development work, the two individuals identified their temperament preferences as Artisan and Guardian.

The Guardian got angry with the Artisan, who did what she felt was appropriate in specific situations. The Guardian felt the Artisan was ignoring the agreed-upon process. The Artisan got impatient with the Guardian, who seemed to always do things "by the book," and she felt the Guardian showed no flexibility.

The resolution was for both to understand their skill-set differences. By recognizing their differences, they were able to discuss situations and together determine whether adaptability or consistency was best to produce the tangible outcomes needed.

A COLLISION OF LOGISTICS AND DIPLOMACY

The way out of the logistics-diplomacy collision is to agree on roles.

Logistics
Procedures and
Approaches

Focus on
preserving the
group

Diplomacy
Team members
actualizing their
potential

Focus on
providing for a
unique identity

Example: A junior member of a team (a Guardian) got caught up in the logistics and procedures of preparing for a major client meeting. A more senior team member (an Idealist) interpreted the Guardian's attention to procedural details as a lack of concern about creating a space for people to grow and develop.

Their difference came to a head in the client meeting when the Idealist snapped at the Guardian for insisting on following the agenda when the Idealist felt the group needed to discuss deeper issues. The Guardian felt awful because she was just trying to be helpful, but she didn't say anything.

After the meeting, the Idealist brought up the situation to resolve the issue. They agreed on which roles they would take in the future and agreed on a signal to let each other know when each saw a need for his or her own role.

SAME TEMPERAMENT COLLISIONS

The skill-set collisions can also occur within the same temperament skill set: tactics versus tactics, logistics versus logistics, strategy versus strategy, diplomacy versus diplomacy.

- Artisan Tactics—Seeing different tactical actions as needed
- Guardian Logistics—Having different logistical plans in mind
- Rational Strategy—Envisioning divergent strategies
- Idealist Diplomacy—Focusing on different issues to resolve diplomatically

The way out of all these conflicts is to appreciate the commonalities and find areas of shared interest. The Bridging Differences tool on page 176 and the Shared Interest Worksheet on page 177 will help resolve collisions of approaches.

Core Values

When core needs or values are threatened, conflict can emerge. Understanding what each temperament values in others can be helpful.

IDEALIST	GUARDIAN
• Values and respects others' ideals. • Values and respects people being authentic.	• Values and respects others' rules. • Values and respects "the way" of doing things.
RATIONAL	ARTISAN
• Values and respects others' expertise. • Values and respects the search for truths.	• Values and respects others' skillful performances. • Values and respects the other as an equal.

On remote teams it takes longer to see what others value, so team members are less likely to acknowledge these values.

Example: A remote team of five (two Rationals, two Guardians, one Idealist) was asked to take on a project. One of the Rationals, one of the Guardians, and the Idealist had worked together very successfully in the past.

The new team struggled from the first meeting. Each of the Rationals followed a different model of how to go about the work. Each had done separate research and had developed a strategy to bring to the group. Neither valued the other's expertise. The Guardians didn't help resolve the issue as each was aligned with a different Rational. The Idealist had a quiet way of interacting and he didn't employ his diplomacy skills.

The team met face to face just once a month to work on the project. Between meetings, no progress was made since there was no agreement on the strategy. This lengthened the Storming stage.

Finally, the Idealist spoke and encouraged the team to talk about the issue. The team did so and decided to restart and take a fresh approach to the project. That fresh approach jump-started the project, and while the team delivered its solution late, the solution they delivered was of excellent quality.

Beginning again with a new approach helped resolve the conflict of core values as well as the collision of conflicting strategies.

Time Orientation

The four temperaments have different time orientations, which can cause conflict.

On a remote team, if a person on a conference call is frustrated, it may be easier for him or her to drop out of the conversation and do other work than to press the team to deal with the frustration. When the frustration is not dealt with, it can build to become a bigger concern for the individual and the team.

IDEALIST	GUARDIAN
• Future orientation—the "tomorrow" • Likely to get frustrated when potential is ignored, when no time is spent envisioning an ideal situation, when people dwell on the past and it becomes a roadblock to growth.	• Past orientation—the "then" • Likely to get frustrated when not enough value is given to learning lessons from the past, looking at what's come before, or using what is known to have worked in the past.
RATIONAL	ARTISAN
• Infinite orientation—the "timeless" • Likely to get frustrated when the team doesn't look at how the past relates to the future in determining immediate actions, and when the team ignores universal principles and truths.	• Present orientation—the "now" • Likely to get frustrated by too much focus on "how it was," "how it could be," or "how it all relates to everything else."

Evaluating Solutions

In evaluating solutions or approaching decisions, people of different temperaments will focus on different aspects of an issue.

IDEALIST	GUARDIAN
• Will the solution promote growth and development?	• How is the solution useful?
RATIONAL	ARTISAN
• What are the pragmatic consequences of the solution?	• Is the solution relevant?

On a remote team, be sure to take time to check that these questions are answered for each team member. This is important for co-located teams as well, but easier for remote teams to skip due to the time pressure of conference calls.

Example: A team of four (an Artisan, a Guardian, a Rational, and an Idealist) was charged with finding new office space. Each person had different concerns and areas of focus in solving the problem—finding the right space.

The Artisan called a broker right away to find out what was available. He wanted to look at spaces individually and then inform the team of those he thought would be workable. The Rational thought of all the criteria involved in fulfilling the need. She also wanted to be sure the space would support the business growth that was planned. The Idealist was concerned about the impact of moving too far away from where each employee lived. She also wanted to be sure the space would provide an environment supportive of people fulfilling their potential and getting work done. The Guardian wanted to be sure the space would meet all the different functional requirements. She was also concerned about finding a space that would be affordable and knowing what add-on costs, including the cost of moving, would be incurred.

At first the team members argued about how to approach the project. They realized they needed to put all concerns on the table to make their process more efficient and to meet all the key needs. They realized that each approach added value to getting them the best office space.

Styles of Learning

The four temperaments represent four different styles of learning. Since learning is critical for successful teams, these differences can cause conflict.

IDEALIST	GUARDIAN
• Identifies with a subject and makes it his or her own • Finds meaning in the subject	• Sees a subject, practices it, uses it, improves it • Understands how the subject relates to what is known
RATIONAL	ARTISAN
• Understands the underlying logic of "it" • Feels that a subject is masterable	• Does what a subject requires • Sees the relevance of the subject

Example: The leader of a small company (an Artisan) has a team of three people (all Guardians) reporting to her. In the past, when the leader had something new she wanted a team member to take on, she would hand it to the person and essentially say, "Just do this."

After learning about temperament differences, the leader has learned that the three team members learn better when they can relate the new work to something they have done before. Now when the leader has a new task, she takes some time to explain how it relates to other tasks and asks questions to help the individuals make the connections.

Everyone is happier. The employees are learning more tasks and learning more quickly. The leader is happy because her employees are more productive and are accomplishing the new tasks she assigns.

When teaching a remote team member something, it's easy to let the communications technology limit your teaching to a different style than your own or the learner's. Ask what the learner needs and adapt!

Approaches to Tasks and Relationships

Different temperaments approach relationships and tasks differently, providing another source of potential conflict.

IDEALIST	GUARDIAN
Relationship centered • Checks in with others regarding a vision of the ideal • Focuses on interconnectedness • Wants unity and authenticity	Authority centered • Finds steadiness in statement of purpose, guidelines, protocols, plans • Focuses on having an approach • Wants accountability, measures, and records
RATIONAL	ARTISAN
Knowledge centered • Asks why? how? how to? and why? again • Focuses on ingenuity and new knowledge • Wants a deep understanding	Impact centered • Shifts team energy through wit and banter • Focuses on action • Wants products to be impactful

Polarities

A common view is that there must be a right and a wrong in an issue. In the case of polarities, both sides have a contribution to make.

Barry Johnson provided this definition in his book *Polarity Management*: "Polarities...are sets of opposites which can't function well independently. Because the two sides of a polarity are interdependent, you can't choose one as a solution and neglect the other." [13]

Temperament dynamics give us three sets of polarities:

1. Language
2. Role assumptions
3. Interest and focus

LANGUAGE POLARITY

Language provides us with a way to think about things, a way to translate back and forth between our thoughts, feelings, and world-views and the events and people in our world. Our language usually reflects our natural way of viewing the world. Language can be classified as two kinds—abstract and concrete. Abstract and concrete language are explained in chapter 5. We repeat the information here for your application.

Abstract language is the polar opposite of concrete language. Good communication involves both, yet by our natural tendencies, we tend to prefer one kind over the other.

Abstract Language

Abstract language describes abstractions, concepts, and patterns, referencing only as much sensory detail as needed. This is the language of implications, hypotheses, or symbolic meanings. It references what is theoretical, not applied or practical. There is usually little reference to specific situations, instances, or experiences. Abstract language is the language of choice to describe what exists mainly in the mind and an envisioned ideal world. This language describes a "reality" that is not easily "seen," but is just as real as the tangible world.

Those with a preference for the Idealist temperament often use global and impressionistic abstract language so people can make their own meanings and find their own identities. In the Rational temperament pattern, abstract language is usually more precise and specific with the goal of increased clarity leading to knowledge.

Concrete Language

Concrete language describes tangible realities backed up by sensory observations. The goal of concrete language is to make things more "real" or specific. It describes what exists, existed, or will exist in reality and is perceptible to the senses. It may stand for an object as it exists in nature, not the abstracted attributes of that object. It relates to material things by reviewing events, facts, images, memories, and how things look, feel, taste, and sound.

For those with a preference for the Guardian temperament, concrete language often references past events, sequences of events, how one fact is linked to another, or physical responses to past events. For the Artisan temperament, concrete language is used to heighten awareness of physical reality by vivid, sensory descriptions of immediate or near-future events or experiences, often in a random fashion that creates a tangible image in the mind of the listener.

	ABSTRACT LANGUAGE	CONCRETE LANGUAGE
Focus On	• Intangibles—concepts, ideas, implications, and meanings	• Tangibles—experiences and observations
Intent	• To know or explain the meaning of something that is not seen in order to access information that is not obvious	• To get or give useful, concrete information to plan for the future or take action in the present
Behavior	• Ask questions to get meaning or logic and understand patterns • Often use metaphors and speak symbolically • Talk about intuitions and insights	• Ask questions to get details or see a pattern • Often use analogies and reference the facts • Talk about hunches and gut reactions
Comfort Zone	• Introspection • What is ideal • Ideas, conjecture, conceptualizing, envisioning, and figurative expressions	• Observation • What is real • Firsthand experiences and descriptions of actual events or situations

	Abstract Language	Concrete Language
Examples	• "Her purpose in life is…" • "I think we need to examine this data in relation to the larger systems issues." • "In a situation, I'm always thinking about what I'm thinking and what they're thinking and how the context is influencing us and wondering how what they're thinking about me is influencing them…"	• "She says she wants to be a…" • "Here is the data that shows just where the system is breaking down." • "In a situation, my focus is to stay in touch with what is happening or what I am doing and experiencing and what they're doing and experiencing…"
Tendencies	• Often see reality as arbitrary • Seek concepts and meanings to focus on details—impatient with concrete details in isolation	• Often see ideas as arbitrary • Seek details about the pieces to build concepts and patterns—impatient when concepts, patterns, and theories are presented alone

With both kinds of language, the individual wants the other person to see or understand what he or she sees or understands.

When two people are having a conversation and find they are not understanding each other, it may be due to a difference between concrete and abstract language. Each wants the other to see what he or she sees but may feel that the other is dismissing his or her reality and that therefore, the agenda behind the language is not being understood or met.

	THE PERSON USING ABSTRACT LANGUAGE	THE PERSON USING CONCRETE LANGUAGE
Desires	• To push the other to look at possibilities and potentials	• To raise an awareness of the actuality
Is likely to	• Look for a framework or purpose to connect to data	• Give more data to clarify
Shares	• Something and there is more	• Something and it feels done
May say	• "There's more than meets the eye."	• "It is what it is."
Triggers defensiveness by...	• Sharing ideas: the other person may feel stupid in not being able to get a picture of the idea.	• Asking questions to flesh out the details: the other person may see the questions as attacks or challenges.

The solution here is for both communicators to "come to the same side of the table." In other words, work together to see the issue from one person's view and then from the other's view.

On a remote team, language polarity is amplified because the options we often use in face-to-face meetings are missing. Also, when we are remote, we can't see that the implications we make aren't being received by the other person or that the data doesn't connect in a meaningful or useful way for the other as it does for us.

When a person who prefers abstract language senses that he or she is not communicating in a way that's working for the person who prefers concrete language, the speaker may pause to find new words—on the telephone, the pause isn't easy to read and may be misinterpreted.

When someone with a preference for concrete language senses that he or she is not communicating well with a person who prefers abstract language (possibly because there is no feedback), the speaker may switch to asking questions to clarify. These questions may be perceived as condescending and may even result in even more detail, thus making it worse.

When we are face to face, we often notice the miscommunication sooner and can deal with it sooner. When together, we can draw pictures, chart key points or ideas, and use gestures and body language to communicate our ideas. Unless we have a computer "white board" application or a video screen available to us during our remote conversation, we lose the benefits these approaches can provide.

Solutions for bridging language polarities include the following:

- Recognize each person's language type preference.
- Ask for clarification when you aren't clear what the other person is talking about.
- Ask questions to see if your understanding matches the speaker's intention (active listening skills).
- Make space for the other person's language (allow him or her to speak without judgment).

Language polarity conflict comes up not just when we speak, but also in other forms of communication. Watch your e-mail messages: are you using language that will connect with your audience?

A person we know who has a tendency to use concrete language says, "It's not concrete enough until I can see a picture in my head."

A person we know who has a tendency to use abstract language says, "I can't see details until I have a conceptual overview."

Example: A Guardian (who preferred concrete languge) and an Idealist (who preferred abstract language) were having a discussion. The Guardian kept asking questions such as "How are you going to do that?" and "What does it look like?" and "What do you mean by that?"

The Idealist was thinking, "He doesn't like my ideas" and "Why is he attacking me? I thought it was a good idea." When the Idealist asked the Guardian why he was attacking her, the Guardian replied, "I get a sense of your enthusiasm, but I can't get a picture of what your idea looks like and how we're going to make it happen." Once the Idealist realized the questions were clarifying questions rather than criticizing questions, she relaxed and was able to come up with some concrete details.

ROLE ASSUMPTION POLARITY

Another type of polarity conflict is that of role assumption. When people come together to accomplish something, typically either they first consider the team or team members and strive to get the job done together in an affiliative manner, or they refer to the desired outcome and more autonomously take whatever action they see fit to produce the outcome in a pragmatic manner. These are the two major kinds of roles we take in our interactions: affiliative or pragmatic. The affiliative and pragmatic roles are polar opposites. Engaging in one to the exclusion of the other leads to team failure. Affiliative and pragmatic roles are explained in chapter 5. We repeat the information here for your application.

Affiliative Roles

Affiliative roles require that people act in community, with a sense of what is good for the team. They may be people or task focused. They may be practical or idealistic. No matter what, there is always some sense of cooperation and interdependence. In this way of interacting, it is important to have roles defined, to get agreement.

	AFFILIATIVE ROLES	PRAGMATIC ROLES
Focus	• Interdependence • Human and team effectiveness	• Independence • Effectiveness
Intent	• Inclusion	• Self-determination
Behavior	• Cooperative activities • Seeking agreement • Sanction: checking in with norms and values	• Autonomous actions • Seeking outcomes • Expedience: choosing actions to meet goals
Comfort Zone	• Well-defined roles • People cooperating and getting along	• Freedom to engage in expedient actions regardless of roles • People focusing on excellence in performance
Examples	• Mary checked with Dan about being off campus for a workshop. • Is this decision okay with you? • I usually ask for permission first.	• Mary informed Dan she would be off campus for a workshop. • Can you live with this decision? • I often ask for forgiveness later.
Tendencies	• Uneasy when people don't work together toward a goal. • Often surprised when people resist defining roles and ignore role assignments. • May be frustrated by what appears to be lack of cooperation. • May be seen as too "other centered."	• Uneasy when roles are decided for them. • Often surprised when people are offended by their independent actions. • May be frustrated by what seem to be roadblocks to expedient action. • May be seen as too independent.

For those with a preference for the Guardian pattern, affiliative roles have clear lines of responsibility and authority. This makes it easy to know where they belong and how they fit in. The concern is to maintain the team. For the Idealist pattern, affiliative roles help them know who they are, their unique identity, and provide a way to find meaning and purpose in what they do.

Pragmatic Roles

Pragmatic roles require that individuals act in accordance with what they see needs to be done to get the desired result. They, too, may be people or task focused. They, too, may be practical or idealistic. When a decision needs to be made or an action needs to be taken, their first inclination is to act more independently regardless of norms or consensus. In this way of interacting, individual autonomy is very important.

For those with a preference for the Artisan pattern, pragmatic roles give the freedom and autonomy to act according to the needs of the moment. For the Rational pattern, pragmatic roles ensure a focus on the overall strategy and vision and give a sense of mastery and self-control.

The person with a pragmatic preference will use the affiliative approach when it's pragmatic to do so. For example, that person will use consensus building with a team if it's expedient in getting the job done.

PEOPLE IN AFFILIATIVE ROLES	PEOPLE IN PRAGMATIC ROLES
• "What is my role?" • Follow the rules • Get permission or consent • "Is it okay with you?" • "Does it follow the rules?"	• "I'm going to do it my way." • Design without input • Fail to respond to questions • "I'm going to take action as I see needed." • "Strategically, here's what we need to go with this."

The person with an affiliative preference will use a pragmatic approach when he or she has permission or consent. For example, if the team members all agree that an individual can make a decision on specific issues—in other words, the areas of autonomy are clearly defined—then the affiliative person will more comfortably agree to the independent decision making.

Example: In an organization of about 50 people, the leadership team consists of the following officers:

- Chief Executive Officer (CEO): Artisan
- Chief Operations Officer (COO): Rational
- Chief Financial Officer (CFO): Guardian
- VP of Human Resources (VPHR): Guardian
- VP of Marketing (VPM): Idealist

The group has worked together for a year or so. Early in its work together, the team developed guidelines for operating together. Those guidelines included agreeing to make decisions as a group.

The CEO and COO (both pragmatic) often go ahead and do things according to what they see needs to be done, rather than getting agreement with the other three team members first. The CFO, VPHR, and VPM (all affiliative) are frustrated by this tendency of the CEO and the COO, but in order to maintain relationships and/or to honor the team hierarchy, they don't bring up the issue of not adhering to the agreed-on norms. Thus the CFO and COO don't get the feedback that would help them adjust their behavior when needed.

The VPM is the third person in that position in three years. The VPHR is looking for a job outside the company. The CFO "isn't really there." She's doing only what's necessary.

The team needs to discuss the conflict, and recognize the need to act without consensus at times, and adjust the norms because unless the conflict is resolved, the team will split apart.

The affiliative-pragmatic polarity is tough on teams in remote work environments. It's easier for individual team members to be pragmatic and autonomous since they don't feel the presence of the others. It's also easier for members to misread each other as uncaring or selfish. To be affiliative in the remote environment takes extra effort to find people, schedule time to talk, and so on. It also takes time for all the members to connect to a purpose, get input, ask about feelings, and review team progress. So some or all of the team affiliative activities might get skipped, and those activities are often precisely what pulls a team together. Without them, the team then acts with less interdependence and loses the ability to gain synergistic solutions.

The extremes of interaction don't work well in teams. If a team operates too pragmatically, it can easily become a "do good" team. If a team operates with too much affiliativeness, it can easily become a "feel good" team. (See page 18–19 for more on "do good" and "feel good" teams.)

Tips:

- Don't assume that those with a pragmatic preference will not be team players. They may come to see interdependence as the most pragmatic mode for teamwork.
- Don't assume that because people are affiliative they will be team players. They can still be self-absorbed.

Realize that, paradoxically, people can become more interdependent if they are given space for independence. The lesson here is about balance—not allowing too much of either approach.

INTEREST AND FOCUS POLARITY

Yet another polarity conflict comes from where different people focus their attention or interest. We can focus our attention on different things. Often in our communications we find our interest and attention going to either the structure of a situation or to people's motives. Conflict can often result from having a different focus and thus promoting different actions. Guardians and Rationals tend to focus more on structure, and Idealists and Artisans tend to focus more on motives. As with the other polarities, if we ignore one to the exclusion of the other, something important might get neglected. Interest and focus are explained in chapter 5. We repeat the information here for your application.

Structure

For those with a preference for the Guardian temperament pattern, the interest in structure is concrete and procedural. Guardian structures provide rules, norms, roles, and responsibilities. Examples include sequential outlines, family trees, and organizational charts. These structures serve to inform others about what is appropriate and what can be expected.

In the Rational pattern, the structural attention goes to the abstract and multidimensional, as in logic and matrices, coordinates, and organizing principles. Rational structures provide implementation strategies, and at the same time they provide ways to catalogue and master the principles of how the world operates. The goal is for all to learn to be more competent and efficient within the system.

Motive

For those with a preference for the Artisan temperament pattern, attention is paid first to what an individual "gets" out of a situation. Motives are the reasons people do things. They must be paid attention to in order to get the desired results. Knowing a person's motives provides the Artisan cues to freely respond as the other person pursues his or her wants and needs.

In the Idealist temperament pattern, attention goes to others' meaning and purpose of being. For Idealists, motives represent a person's spirit and higher purpose in life. Motives must be attended to because they provide opportunities to achieve consensus and to work together toward a common goal and at the same time achieve a purpose.

	ATTENTION TO STRUCTURE	ATTENTION TO MOTIVE
Focus	• Order and organization	• Why people do things
Intent	• To have a measure of control over life's problems	• To have a way to work with people rather than trying to force them into a preconceived structure
Behavior	• Ask or wonder about how things are organized or sequenced • Notice and refer to methods and requirements or rules	• Ask or wonder what is motivating someone • Notice and refer to "what's in it" for the other person
Comfort Zone	• When the order of things is clear	• When others' motives are clear
Examples	• "Here, this might help. I've outlined…" • "Where do we start?" • "Let's be careful and systematic about this…"	• "What was really going on with her was…" • "Why did he do…?" • "What's in it for them is…"
Tendencies	• Detecting the details of the content of a communication and missing the real purpose behind a behavior	• Detecting the purpose behind a behavior and missing pieces of the content of a communication

Teams need to focus on both structure and motive. If a team focuses only on structure, it may miss what drives people. If the team focuses only on motive, it may miss achieving results that last.

People with a structure focus will say, "Thinking about motive is a waste of time." The response from those with a motive focus will be "You're missing something important." People with a motive focus may say, "Structure isn't necessary." The response from those with a structure focus will be "Without structure, we won't get the work done."

If the focus is mostly on structure, team members may miss

- That people in the team are feeling conflict
- The reasons behind the conflict
- Why people are doing particular things

If the focus is mostly on motives, team members may

- See conflict where there is none
- Miss the point of a discussion or action

The way out of the structure-motive conflict is to focus on the positive aspects of both:

- Structure helps to keep the team from missing necessary aspects of the task or project.
- Motive helps the team notice performance issues.
- Structure gives the team a path or method to follow.
- Motive helps maximize individual contributions by tapping into what drives them.

Focusing on the positive aspects of both structure and motive creates a healthier team with a path that maximizes team members' contributions.

On a remote team, sorting through conflict over motives and structure should not be done via e-mail. This is an important time for conversation.

Needs from Leader

The Storming stage can be very unpleasant for some team members, and there is a danger that they will opt out of the team if they can. It is critical, therefore, for the team leader to actively help the team get through the Storming stage. To do this, the leader must perform the following tasks:

- Facilitate conflict resolution
- Accept and understand differences
- Support and encourage participation
- Acknowledge difficulties
- Encourage two-way communication
- Reinforce commitment
- Facilitate decision making

IDEALISTS	GUARDIANS
Want to know that… • We'll come out on the other side of storming intact. • The leader will build bridges among the factions. • The leader will turn disagreements into dialogue. • The leader will surface the discontents.	Want to know that… • Something practical and useful will come of storming. • The leader is managing the process. • The leader is providing a structure for working through the Storming stage. • The leader is sharing a framework for the storming process.
RATIONALS	ARTISANS
Want to know that… • What comes out of storming will make logical sense. • The leader is competent and is strategically handling the storming. • The leader is sharing a framework for the storming process. • The leader will honor each member's own competency.	Want to know that… • Opportunities won't be missed and the storming process will pay off. • The leader will stimulate the team to action. • The leader will be brave enough to weather the storm. • The leader will navigate a way through the storming process.

If the team does not have a formal leader, this is the time to call in someone from outside who can ensure the above actions get taken.

All the team members need a sense that the leader can get them through the Storming stage. What each member is looking for specifically is temperament related.

Remote team leaders: be sure you are communicating what you are doing so that team members of each temperament know specifically how you will help the team.

Worst Fears

The leader must manage the worst fears of each temperament represented on the team.

	Worst fear is...	Leader needs to...
Artisan	• Inaction will rule and the team will accomplish nothing.	• Not let discussions go too long without articulating actions to be taken.
Guardian	• Chaos will rule and it will keep the team from being efficient and effective.	• Set up and/or adhere to agreed upon operating guidelines.
Rational	• Emotion will rule and the team will drown in the emotion.	• Use a calm, reasonable tone of voice.
Idealist	• Argumentiveness will rule and the team will reach no resolution.	• Manage disagreements and focus on points of agreement along the way.

Actions to Move through the Storming Stage

Being face to face is the most desirable position in which to work out conflict. If that's not possible, working voice to voice is a much better alternative than e-mail. Pick a time, set up a meeting, and then work through the conflict.

In the Forming chapter, we identified key actions relating to the task or relationship dimensions of teamwork (or both). As a team grows and becomes more complex, even seemingly task-oriented actions contribute to relationship building. Therefore, we won't identify the actions below as specifically task or relationship oriented.

Six key actions can help the team move through the Storming stage. Since the team is still unable to lead itself, it is the responsibility of the leader to engage the team in these conversations and in the use of appropriate tools to work through conflicts.

1. Reinforce forming actions.
2. Develop skills.
3. Clarify working processes.
4. Revisit dialoguing on differences to bridge those differences.
5. Focus on clarity of communication.
6. Focus on shared interests.

1. Reinforce Forming Actions

Revisiting the team goal, roles, and norms or operating guidelines to be sure they are still relevant and that everyone is on the same page can be useful. Those with a pragmatic preference tend to resist norm setting. Those with an affiliative preference may be more concerned about roles, norms, and operating procedures than goals. Don't let resistance keep you from taking this important step.

2. Develop Skills

By focusing the team (and individuals) on building the skills needed to do the work, the leader can get everyone contributing to the team goal.

If common skills are needed by multiple team members, there may be some ways to have members learn together. If a team member has skills that others need, mentoring and/or teaching relationships can be set up.

Consider using the Team Skills Audit (page 174) as a vehicle for team conversation on current skills and talents.

3. Clarify Working Processes

Different ideas on how to best accomplish tasks or projects are often a source of conflict in teams. Sharing work products and clarifying working processes can be very useful in getting the needed common processes in place.

From a temperament view, understanding the affiliative and pragmatic approaches (pages 116–120) to tasks can also help in clarifying processes. Recognize that those with a pragmatic preference are likely to want fewer formal role and process descriptions, while those with an affiliative preference take comfort in having the working processes clarified. You may need to reframe the work descriptions in pragmatic terms. Having processes clarified and outlined usually makes the team more efficient.

On remote teams, it's not always obvious that people are using different approaches.

4. Revisit Dialoguing on Differences

Differences in approaches and in personality are going to surface in the team. A good team leader can facilitate a discussion to get the issues on the table and focus the team on the strengths that each person has to contribute.

This chapter on temperament and storming can help the team understand how differences in temperament might be contributing to current conflict. If the conflict concerns the whole team, consider the Map the Team II tool on page 175. If the conflict seems to be just between individuals, the Bridging Differences tool on page 176 may be more helpful.

5. Focus on Clarity of Communication

Communication is critical for teams—particularly remote teams. It's worth spending time clarifying what gets communicated to whom, when, and via what technology. Review the communication guidelines established in the Forming stage as appropriate.

From a temperament view, understanding the abstract and concrete uses of language can help in clarifying communication. See pages 111–116 for details on this polarity and ideas on how to resolve any conflict.

6. Focus on Shared Interests Using the Sustainable Resolution Model

One key way to resolve conflict or differences is to focus on shared interests or shared goals. When people in conflict identify their shared goals, the dialogue proceeds something like the following diagram: [14]

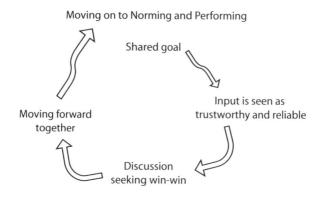

Moving on to Norming and Performing

Shared goal

Input is seen as trustworthy and reliable

Discussion seeking win-win

Moving forward together

If the parties involved can articulate their shared goal, then as the dialogue proceeds, the input from each party tends to be seen as trustworthy and reliable since it should support the shared goal. This confidence leads to an interest in discussion that will seek a win-win solution to the disagreement. As a solution is agreed on, the parties can move forward together. The result is a common solution and a reinforcement of the shared goal. Norming and Performing teams tend to use this model. It generates productive dialogue.

Storming teams are more likely to use a different process, which starts with conflicting goals and suppresses dialogue.[15]

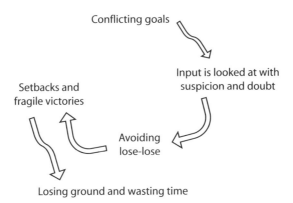

When the parties start a discussion with conflicting goals, then any input is likely to be looked on with suspicion and doubt. Even if one person says something that sounds supportive of the opposite position, the support is likely to be discounted since the person's true goal is known. The parties generally prefer to avoid getting into a discussion since each has an opposing view. Solutions may be reached (often by default), yet these solutions are fragile, and as soon as something goes wrong, the parties will say something like "I told you so!" and dig deeper into their own positions. In this way, the parties lose ground and are further from coming together than before.

Storming teams often operate in this way. It sends them into a downward spiral that is tough to recover from. The solution? Ask a key question that will identify a shared goal and move the conversation to the shared-goal model above.

This matrix is another way to look at what the Sustainable Resolution Model says:

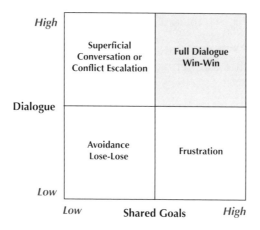

The "frustration" box is the box of opportunity—the opportunity to move into full dialogue and a win-win resolution. The frustration is due to the lack of dialogue. Shared goals aren't articulated in a common language (abstract or concrete), or the focus on differences overrides the desire to understand each other.

Moving on to the Norming Stage

Teams can and do get through the Storming stage—some more easily than others. Conflict doesn't always get resolved, however understanding others' needs, values, and talents can increase our tolerance for the differences and help us move forward together. Members are likely to emerge from the Storming stage with increased knowledge of themselves, each other, and the work to be done. This prepares them for the Norming stage and more productive work together.

Be aware, your team may fall back into the Storming stage if conflicts have not been properly dealt with.

Let's look again at the software development team (one Idealist, two Rationals, and one Artisan) that we talked about at the end of chapter 4, Forming (page 89). As the team members grew more comfortable using their natural talents, the differences between two key team members became more apparent, and unresolved conflicts began pushing the team frequently back to storming. The differing members had built a good deal of mutual trust and respect by this point, but they were in danger of losing it. They both knew they should sit down and work through the frustrations their differences were creating, but they also felt there was more trust and team cohesion than ever before, and they didn't want to risk losing that.

So they procrastinated having the discussion, and the problem grew worse. At that point, the leader of the company stepped in and asked to facilitate a discussion of differences. He ensured that all frustrations were surfaced and worked through. He left halfway through the meeting, when it was clearly going well.

By the end of the meeting, the team members had connected at a deeper level than ever before. In addition, the next week resulted in some of the most significant breakthroughs in the history of the team. Upon examination, these breakthroughs were found to be the direct result of the two members connecting their very different ideas into one cohesive plan—a norming process that began at the facilitated meeting.

NORMING

8

Understanding Temperament and the Norming Stage

When a team reaches the Norming stage of development, it's usually working together pretty well. Norming doesn't need to take a lot of team time and shouldn't be laborious. If it is taking your team a lot of time and effort, you are probably still in the Storming stage and avoiding dealing with some important issues.

Which of the following characteristics are true for your norming team?

CHARACTERISTIC	TRUE FOR MY TEAM
Feelings of relief and confidence	
A sense of team cohesion	
Development of harmony, trust, support, and respect	
Acknowledgment of member contributions	
Evidence of real progress toward goals	
More openness and feedback	
Use of a team language	

It's very easy to get settled into this comfortable stage, and the danger of settling in can be groupthink. Groupthink is a mode of thinking that people engage in when their striving for unanimity overrides their motivation to realistically appraise alternative courses of action.

Settling-In Dangers

The likely reasons for falling into groupthink vary by temperament.

IDEALIST	GUARDIAN
• Gets enamored with the peace and mutuality	• Gets stuck in a sense of stability
RATIONAL	ARTISAN
• Gets too comfortable exercising current competencies	• Gets settled into adapting to the team or performing needed tasks

Assumptions about the Team

A norming team follows both written and unwritten norms. The danger is that the unwritten norms don't get addressed openly. Unwritten norms often constrain the team because they are not challenged when the team is unproductive. Violation of unwritten norms can throw the team back into storming.

For example, team members begin to assume that someone will take a particular role because that person has taken that role in the past.

IDEALIST	**GUARDIAN**
• Everyone's well intended. I can connect with everyone.	• Everyone's fulfilling their responsibilities. I know what my role is.
RATIONAL	**ARTISAN**
• Everyone's competent. I'm free to do what I think needs to be done.	• Everyone will do their part. I'm free to take the actions I see need to be taken.

MEMBERS ARE SURPRISED WHEN . . .

IDEALIST	**GUARDIAN**
• I don't have the connection I thought I had or others don't turn out to be the way I thought they were.	• Other people expect me to do other things or they encroach on my role.
RATIONAL	**ARTISAN**
• Others don't act autonomously or they don't respect my competence.	• I'm not as free as I thought or sanctions get imposed when others don't do their part.

Remote Team Concerns

Members of a remote norming team may also make assumptions that everything is okay and may check in with each other less often than they did while forming or managing conflict. Because they don't see each other, remote team members run a higher risk than co-located team members experiencing the surprises on the previous page.

Needs from Leader

The norming team has little need for the leader to be "hands on." The real role of the leader at this stage is to watch for leverage points during norming and then to create the right environment for the team to move quickly into performing.

	LEVERAGE POINT	LEADER NEEDS TO PROVIDE OPPORTUNITY FOR...
Artisan	• Gets bored	• Increased variety and excitement
Guardian	• Gets discouraged	• Utilization of personal contributions
Rational	• Gets complacent	• Progress and increased personal and team mastery
Idealist	• Gets apathetic	• Renewed meaning and meaning for the team as a group

Example: Our software development team (one Idealist, two Rationals and one Artisan) works as a self-managing team; however, the leader of the organization provides leadership as needed. The team members have been working together for several months. They worked through some storming, when the leader helped the Rationals gain an increased sense of individual mastery as well as a sense of team mastery. He helped the Idealist find renewed meaning in his work and the Artisan feel the excitement of being given the freedom to troubleshoot. The leader noticed new energy, increased efficiency, and improved morale as the team moved into the Norming stage.

Actions to Maximize the Norming Stage

We recommend these six actions to help the norming team move forward:

1. Share leadership.
2. Give and receive feedback.
3. Deepen skills and understanding.
4. Seek input from outside the team.
5. Share opinions and skills.
6. Examine team functioning.

1. Share Leadership

Mature teams have the ability to share leadership and the sharing often happens without anyone specifically saying, "I'll lead this part" or "Would you lead this, Joe?" The sharing just happens as the need for leadership on a project or situation emerges. If one or more members or the leader refuses to give up leadership, the team may be prevented from growing.

For a remote team, growth into shared leadership can be stifled since the fluidity of leadership sharing isn't as simple as it is for a team working face to face. A remote team will probably have to be more explicit about passing leadership among members in order for the sharing to happen.

2. Give and Receive Feedback

While we believe team members should be giving and receiving feedback before the team is at the Norming stage, our experience is that feedback is not often heard and acted on without resentment or defensiveness until this stage. The team members should make sure that giving feedback is a regular part of their conversations.

3. Deepen Skills and Understanding

As the team grows, the need to deepen skills continues to grow too. It's important, particularly in remote situations, to be sure everyone is getting the appropriate skill development.

4. Seek Input from Outside the Team

This is the stage with the highest risk for making groupthink decisions. Groupthink is the propensity for a team to feel that it is invulnerable and to avoid self-censorship.

It's important to check assumptions and conclusions with someone outside the team to ensure that the team isn't engaging in groupthink and therefore making potentially poor decisions.

5. Share Opinions and Skills

When the team gets working at this norming level, it is easy for the members to become complacent and just keep doing what they have been doing. To stay successful and on the leading edge, members need to continue to share opinions and differences. Skills also must be shared so that members can continually learn and be stimulated.

6. Examine Team Functioning

The norming team is in an excellent position to look at how the team is functioning and to adjust in order to make itself better. Whether reexamining processes, guidelines, goals, or relationships, this examination is key to moving past this stage into the Performing stage and high performance. Revisit the tools in the Appendix as needed for help with examining the team.

Moving On to the Performing Stage

The movement from the Norming stage to the Performing stage usually isn't gradual. But team members don't wake up one day and say, "Gee, we're at the next level." More likely, something will trigger the movement forward. The trigger could be relationship oriented—a breakthrough discussion on differences or the result of a team-building session or some other event. Or it might be related to the team's work—again, some kind of breakthrough or success.

Example: Let's revisit our software development team (one Idealist, two Rationals, and one Artisan). The leader of the company decided there was a need to focus on helping the team enhance its sense of purpose. The existing sense of purpose was mostly focused on surviving as this new team and doing what good could be achieved on a difficult project. Now that those goals were no longer so lofty, the leader thought it was time the team refocused on something larger, as he foresaw apathy and complacency quickly setting in otherwise.

The leader scheduled a series of meetings between the team and the CEO of the client company to get the team excited about the client's grand visions and thus instill new and deeper meaning in the team's work. He also frequently spoke to the team and the whole company about his vision of what this team could do. He painted a vivid and compelling picture of an ambitious future, rather than focusing too much on the more basic prior vision of "working well together" and "making the project not suck." This effort included elements that addressed the needs of each of the temperament patterns on the team. The team took hold of a new sense of purpose and a renewed drive for progress, rather than settling in to the comfortable new space they had found in the Norming stage.

PERFORMING

9

Understanding Temperament
and the Performing Stage

We rarely see "performing" teams. Often it's because something
interrupts the team before they can reach this stage of development—a change of goal, completion of the assigned task,
changes in membership, or other change.

One other key reason teams don't reach the performing
stage is that they don't recognize the leverage points that can
propel them to high performance. These leverage points occur
in unrest, which can spur members to drop out or can help to
move the team ahead. We discussed these leverage points in
"Needs from Leader" in chapter 8, "Norming."

Which of the following characteristics are true for your performing team?

Characteristic	True for My Team
A feeling of pride	
Increased output and quality of work	
Shared responsibility	
Collaboration by the whole team and by subgroups	
Close connection of the team members	
Adjustment of roles based on the needs of the team	
Spontaneously emerging leadership	
Shared leadership	
High levels of performance	

Teams that do reach the Performing stage have moved well past allowing differences to be an issue to capitalizing on those differences. To do that, team members need a strong sense of trust.

Trust

Deep trust is what gets the team to the Performing stage and keeps them at this stage. People of each temperament inherently trust different things. They tend to distrust what the other temperaments trust. In a performing team, members make space for those things they would normally distrust.

IDEALIST	GUARDIAN
• Trusts intuition, images, impressions	• Trusts traditions, authority, jurisdiction
RATIONAL	ARTISAN
• Trusts logic, coherence, reason	• Trusts chance, luck, gut feel

Example: Two colleagues (a Rational and an Idealist) were debriefing after an interview that they had conducted together. The Idealist said the interviewee felt a certain way, yet the Rational hadn't heard or seen any logical evidence to indicate that. They had worked together a long time and knew about what each temperament trusts most. This knowledge enabled the Rational to back off from insisting on logic and instead trust the impressions of the Idealist.

Performing teams generally don't find remoteness to be a concern or a limiting factor. Their teamwork transcends the concerns of distance and time.

ENGAGING AT A PERFORMING LEVEL

IDEALIST	GUARDIAN
• The opportunity to be part of something profoundly meaningful supercedes the fear of loss of identity.	• The opportunity to participate in a team that delivers something outstanding supercedes the fear of instability.
RATIONAL	ARTISAN
• The opportunity to do something ingenious supercedes the fear of incompetence or failure.	• The opportunity to do something really impressive supercedes the fear of loss of freedom.

Actions to Maximize the Performing Stage

These four actions can be useful for a performing team:
1. Promote sharing and collaboration among teams
2. Deal promptly with interpersonal and team issues
3. Continue to deepen knowledge and skills
4. Make efficient use of time

1. Promote Sharing and Collaboration among Teams

Once a team has reached the Performing stage, it has an obligation to help others in the organization. This team is in a good position to lead others since it has a track record of success. The motives for helping other teams are the same as those that engage each temperament at this stage (page 143).

2. Deal Promptly with Interpersonal and Team Issues

Issues will continue to come up in the team. It's important to check with other members regularly to be sure issues are being dealt with.

3. Continue to Deepen Knowledge and Skills

Individual and team growth and development will continue to keep members engaged in the work of the team.

4. Make Efficient Use of Time

Team members should look at ways to increase the efficiency of the team's work without impacting the current work or relationships. This is a real opportunity to maximize the team's performance.

Performing: What to Do When It Ends

At some point, the life of the team will end—often because the work is done or members move on to other opportunities. It's worthwhile to note the ending of the team in some way. We know from all that has been written about change that when something ends, people can more easily move forward when they have a chance to say good-bye to what was. This observance can take many forms. Some that we've seen are

- A team lunch or dinner with time to share memories
- A meeting where large sheets of paper are posted on the walls and team members draw their memories
- A celebration after work
- A forum where each member gives feedback to every other member

Be creative. Take time to say good-bye and thank-you, and celebrate your success together.

SECTION IV

SPECIAL
TEAM
CONSIDERATIONS

REMOTE TEAM COMMUNICATION

10

Remote teams can experience communication difficulties in part because it is so difficult to share much information about each other as described using the Johari Window in chapter 3 (page 33). The remote group must make a commitment to sharing information to facilitate communication.

Remote teams communicate in a variety of ways. Below are a few tips for communicating with team members of different temperaments in different situations. (These tips apply to co-located teams as well.)

IDEALISTS	GUARDIANS
• Need to understand how the new information will impact shared understanding and ways of working.	• Need to understand how the new information fits with past efforts.
RATIONALS	ARTISANS
• Need to understand the difference that the new information makes to the team strategy.	• Need to understand the current utility of the new information.

With these different needs in mind, you'll want to be sure all the aspects are covered in your communication, whether it's by e-mail, voice mail, conference call, or e-meeting.

Meetings

Remote meetings can be held in a variety of ways—conference calls, video conferences, e-meetings, and so on. However the meeting is convened, team members of each temperament have specific need requirements that will enable them to participate in a useful and meaningful way.

IDEALISTS	GUARDIANS
• Need agreed-upon ground rules for discussion and decision making, and a collaborative mindset.	• Need a structured agenda with specific time frames and roles.
RATIONALS	ARTISANS
• Need a rationale for the meeting and clear meeting goals.	• Need reasons to attend and clear action outcomes.

Take the time to consider these needs and provide helpful information to team members in a document prior to the remote meeting. You will find team members much more willing to engage when these needs are met.

Feedback

As we know from the Johari Window on page 33, feedback is important for teams. Feedback is critical to remote team members. Without nonverbal cues, team members can be unsure of how they and their work are perceived by others. The remote team should consider ways to meet members' needs for feedback.

Specifically, people of different temperaments need the following types of feedback.

IDEALISTS	GUARDIANS
• Need discerning feedback that affirms the person.	• Need regular and structured feedback on progress against the project plan.
RATIONALS	ARTISANS
• Need situationally relevant feedback to increase competence.	• Need immediate feedback.

The remote environment creates an "out of sight, out of mind" situation. Don't let this keep you from giving regular feedback to each other. Take time on conference calls, or just pick up the phone to give specific feedback.

If you are giving developmental feedback, feedback that has traditionally been called "constructive criticism" or "negative feedback," be sure you do it voice to voice.

Reinforcing feedback, feedback that has traditionally been called "positive feedback," is also best received voice to voice, but other methods are acceptable (e-mail, instant messaging, voice mail, etc.).

EFFECTIVE TEAM LEADERSHIP

11

The team leader can be more effective if he or she uses his or her understanding of temperament differences.

First, it's critical that you as a leader know yourself. Become clear about your own core needs and values and your talents. Knowing yourself well will keep you from imposing your own "be like me" (BLM) agenda on the team and insisting that others do things your way.[16] A danger of BLM is that you unconsciously ignore contributions that are different from yours.

Second, make space for all temperaments to work on the team. Get your own needs and talent agenda out of the way so that people with other temperaments can contribute. You must also be sure that others on the team are allowing the other members to be heard and are valuing their contributions.

Some suggestions for making space for all the temperaments include the following:

- Holding back your own suggestions to let others come forth
- Checking to be sure everyone has had a chance to contribute
- Actively asking those who haven't contributed yet for their input

- Noticing when a conflict may have it roots in a temperament difference and inviting discussion about it using the language of temperament
- Using the concept of managing polarities to keep people with different points of view contributing positively

Third, value and even use the skills of the other temperaments. Don't just lead from your own perspective. Diplomacy, logistics, tactics, and strategy are all necessary for success. If you don't have the skills in these areas, get help from someone who does.

Attending to temperament differences is especially important during project initiation and project closure. It is up to the leader to be sure the following needs are taken into account.

	PROJECT INITIATION	**PROJECT CLOSURE**
Artisans need	• A clear definition of desired outcomes and benefits	• Recognition for their impact and clarity about their next assignment
Guardians need	• A detailed and structured brief that includes roles, task timing, and task sequence	• Recognition for contributions and lessons to build into the next project
Rationals need	• A coherent rationale that shows the project's strategic significance	• Recognition for expert and even ingenious contributions and information about new strategic challenges
Idealists need	• A "map" of the team and their perceptions and understandings: who are the players and how do they see the world?	• Recognition for contributions from their unique strengths and a satisfying transitional process from endings to new beginnings

As the leader, you must lead the team through the stages of development. As we stated in chapter 2, you will need to adjust what you do with and for the team as it grows through the stages. Don't be afraid to take the lead early on. And then be sure to let go when the team needs you to do so.

If your team is remote, you should have a heightened sense of responsibility. Our book *Quick Guide to Interaction Styles and Working Remotely* is a very good tool to help you build relationships with your remote team members, understand further aspects of differences that particularly show up in remote situations, learn how to empower your remote team members, and learn how to effectively measure their performance.

SPECIAL SITUATIONS IN TEAM DEVELOPMENT

12

As you can see, the stages of team development can provide a very useful framework for understanding teams. A few key questions often arise that we discuss here.

Skipping Stages

Some teams feel that they move very quickly to Performing without ever experiencing Storming. Characteristics of these teams include the following:

- A strong, compelling goal
- Excitement
- Tasks that are breaking new ground
- Lots of learning
- A conscious effort to build on differences

We offer two examples of teams where this quick movement to the Performing stage occurred. Each had a different ultimate outcome.

Example A: A team of four people came together to create a facilitator's guide for a five-day workshop. Three of the four temperaments were represented (Rational, Idealist, and Artisan). The group built relationships quickly and delved into the project. The outcome was an outstanding product that is still used several years later.

When the team took on its next project, it didn't experience the same results. Even though the situation was different, the team started as though it was already performing. This approach gave no space for identifying new roles or clarifying the new goal. Many assumptions were made about how the work would be done, and the team quickly found itself storming. They weren't equipped to deal with the Storming stage since they had skipped it before. Ultimately, the project failed.

Example B: A remote team of three people (a Guardian, a Rational, and an Idealist) worked together over a period of six months to create a learning product. The result was twenty-six individual modules for team development that broke new ground in the organization and were widely recognized as very useful for teams.

This team was able to replicate its experience twice more. The members attributed that successful repetition to the good forming work they did each time they started a new project.

The moral of these stories is that while you may be able to move quickly to performing in a particular situation, each time a new project is started, the team needs to recognize the need to re-form and spend sufficient time in the Forming stage.

The Appeal of the Stages to the Temperaments

Looking at the stages and how they relate to the four temperaments, we have noted some interesting observations.

The Forming and Norming stages seem to appeal more to the Guardian and Idealist temperaments. This makes sense given the affiliative nature of these temperaments. These two stages have more to do with building relationships than the other two stages do.

The Storming and Performing stages seem to appeal more to the Artisan and Rational temperaments. This too makes sense given the pragmatic nature of these temperaments. These two stages are more about action, mastery, and progress than the other two stages are. If someone is resisting what is going on at a particular stage, that resistance may provide an insight as to his or her temperament preference.

Changing Membership

Teams do not remain static. The members and the leader can and do change. What does that mean for the stage the team is currently experiencing?

Whether losing or adding members or both, the best teams recognize the impact membership changes can have on the team and specifically take the whole team back to the Forming stage. They do that by taking the following actions:

- Making sure the new person or people get to know all the other team members
- Checking on the team goal (has it changed?)
- Clarifying roles (and changing them as appropriate)
- Clarifying agreed-upon norms and processes (and updating them as needed)
- Sharing techniques for resolving team conflict

Teams that don't purposely go back and revisit the above key areas will likely find the team dragged back to Forming over time. Assumptions about who's doing the work of those who left and about the role of anyone new to the team often cause problems.

The dynamics of a team *will* change. By ignoring the new dynamics, the team is bound to lose ground.

TEAM STRESS

13

Life can be stressful. Let's face it, teamwork can be stressful. And then there is temperament-related stress and remoteness-related stress. These stresses impact team functioning as much or even more than the daily stressors of too much work, illness, life crises, and so on. Both temperament and remote stress can come into play at all stages of team development.

Remote stress is likely to be different for different individuals on the team. Following are a few of the key stressors we've heard remote team members identify:

- Lack of social interaction
- Having to interpret what people are really saying without nonverbal cues
- Delayed feedback
- Being left out of work and/or conversations
- Nonwork interruptions (especially for those working at home)
- Technology challenges (the technology not working or the team member not knowing how to use it effectively)
- Temperament differences as described throughout this book and in this chapter

The primary solution for remote stress is relationship building. Getting to know each other better and then having ways to connect regularly can relieve many of the above stressors or provide a vehicle for expressing the stress and getting a solution from a team member.

Temperament-Related Stress

Temperament-related stress is not the same as the everyday stress of overwork, overindulgence, and worries over money, relationships, and so on. It results from the core needs and values of the temperament pattern not being met. As with most stress, it is worse when we are unaware of its source. Knowledge of your own temperament pattern can help you manage and even prevent such stress.

Team members may be stressed by situations outside the team in which their core needs are not being met. They bring their responses into the work of the team and so may increase storming tendencies. Then interaction within the team may trigger additional temperament stress.

Following is a list of reminders for each temperament about stressors or stress triggers, typical stress behavior, and some ways to help yourself and your teammates.

Artisan

Core Needs

- Freedom to act on the needs of the moment
- Ability to make an impact

Stressors

Artisans are stressed by the continual constraint and limitations on their actions that often happen in work situations that are rule bound. They are also triggered into stress by having to do routine tasks with no challenge or novelty. When they become bored, they have a difficult time mustering the focused attention needed to exercise a skill, which would make them feel that they had impact. And of course, if what they are doing has no impact, Artisans will be stressed.

WHEN STRESSED

When Artisans are stressed, they seek to regain the lost freedom, excitement, and stimulation they so much need. In the milder cases this search takes the form of taking more risks than usual—physical, financial, or social. They may physically ignore the rules or norms and turn their talent for shifting the energy of the group into inappropriate disruptive behavior like cracking jokes, creating a crisis so they can have impact, or creating needless variations and revisions. If the stress is more chronic and they feel trapped and see no way out, the behavior can take the form of retaliation and even sabotage as they find ways around the confining rules and regulations. Unfortunately, these responses to stress often get them assigned more routine jobs and more limitations on their freedom. Artisans under stress can let the team down by following their impulses to do things that are not necessary to the tasks of the team.

ANTIDOTES FOR STRESS

To help Artisans when they are under such stress, let them regain a measure of freedom. Give them a way to vary their activities and thus introduce a little bit of excitement. One Artisan keeps multiple projects going so he can switch when he feels himself getting bored. Help them find options for action and new ways to have impact. Often just doing something with an Artisan and engaging in new activities will help. Other times, they may need to find a challenge that fits the work of the team. They do like to solve problems, so let them take on that more tactical role.

Guardian

Core Needs
- Membership or belonging
- Responsibility or duty

Stressors

Guardians are often triggered into stress by a feeling of not belonging and not being a part of what is going on. They begin to feel abandoned. Insubordination will also trigger stress for them, whether it is the insubordination of others toward them or when they feel they themselves have not given the appropriate recognition to the person in authority. It is also very easy for Guardians to become stressed because they feel they haven't been responsible enough. Their hunger for responsibility can lead them to take on too much responsibility because "someone has to do it."

WHEN STRESSED

Guardians tend to deal with lower levels of stress by complaining. They complain about how things went wrong or are going wrong, how others didn't or don't do their share of the work, how overworked they are, and how things are always changing (and they can't be as responsible as they'd like). As the stress increases they tend to get increasingly sick, exhausted, quietly worried and anxious, or extremely and loudly apologetic. These ways of dealing with the stress provide them with somewhat socially accepted ways of letting go of some of their burdens. Unfortunately, their complaints tend to drive people away and so increase their stress since they get left out of conversations, and they wind up being even more irresponsible as they can't do their work. Guardians may not follow through on their obligations to the team when they feel so overburdened that they become paralyzed.

ANTIDOTES FOR STRESS

To help Guardians who are under such stress, find ways to include them in news and activities. One Guardian noticed he was not following through and not pulling his own weight because he was so tired when he worked on a team where he didn't feel he fit in. He found a way to contribute to the team and feel needed by seeking to define his role more specifically. Guardians often contribute masterful background logistical support, which goes unnoticed unless things go wrong, so be sure to express your appreciation for their contributions and don't pile all the routine tasks onto their shoulders. They take comfort in routine and in predictability, yet they don't always enjoy taking on menial tasks out of a sense of duty and responsibility and then becoming overworked. Be sure to give them permission to take time off and not take on all the work.

Rational

Core Needs

- Mastery and self-control
- Knowledge and competence

Stressors

Rationals get stressed when they feel powerless. They want to have mastery and self-control, so when they feel like they are in a situation where they have no control over what happens or where they feel like they have little will power, they fall into temperament-related stress. They are stressed by their own sense of lacking knowledge or not being smart enough and by feeling incompetent, especially when they lack backup data or their ideas are challenged and they have already been feeling not as smart or capable as their high standards dictate.

WHEN STRESSED

Rationals tend to try to avoid looking at what they don't know, can't do, or don't have mastery over. When they are forced to face the facts of such a situation, they can become obsessed with figuring out or getting evidence for things that are not major. This keeps them occupied with something other than the real issue. They can also become somewhat mindless, forgetting things they know. This mindlessness can show up as mental blocks or word-finding problems, which of course increase stress for Rationals since they don't like to look incompetent and stupid. Rationals may avoid doing something the team wants them to do if they feel incompetent in that task, and then really fail because they did not follow through.

ANTIDOTES FOR STRESS

Helping Rationals out of this kind of stress can be tricky because they can be their own worst critics, and if you give them feedback on their performance and are not an expert in the area, your praise is likely to be discounted. So to help them, you need to find a way for them to experience being competent and knowledgeable. One woman reported that when she was in such a stressed state, her daughter who worked for her would often just happen to come into her office and ask her mother to teach her something. This seemed to get her unstuck. Rationals tend to treat their own stress levels by taking on new projects. Sometimes this is just the thing to gain them a sense of actively applying what they know, and so you may be able to help Rational teammates who are in stress by asking them to help you with a new project. However, too many new projects that a Rational can't get mastery over can put him or her back into a stressed state.

Idealist

Core Needs

- Meaning and significance
- Unique identity

Stressors

Idealists are stressed when they perceive insincerity in others or when they feel they have not been sincere and authentic to themselves. If they sense a lack of integrity in themselves or in others they are working with, they feel betrayed, which worsens the stress. They must have an ideal to believe in and a sense that life has meaning. An environment where they can't find any meaning and significance or where they can't be themselves will trigger their stress response.

WHEN STRESSED

Idealists tend to deal with stress by disassociating. They split their awareness and fool themselves into believing that the situation is different than it is. At these times, they can send "phony selves" out to interact and maintain a semblance of harmony and keep their true selves hidden. Sometimes they take on a role and seem to be dramatically acting out that role rather than being authentic. They may be in such denial about the lack of sincerity on the part of others that they forget they are playing a role and lose themselves in it. Thus the stress response increases the stress. Under such stress Idealists may get so caught up in their self-deception or their loss of identity that they feel incredible shame for not fulfilling their promises to the team.

ANTIDOTES FOR STRESS

You can help Idealists by noticing when they are being a little fake and then seeking to find out if they feel safe to act authentically.

Sometimes all it takes is some affirmation from others that they are appreciated for who they are rather than what they produce. One Idealist posted positive affirmations in her work area to remind herself that who she is counts. Idealists often wind up nurturing others and then don't get enough nurturing themselves, so they have to make time to do the little things for themselves and take time away from empathic relating to re-center themselves. To help Idealists who have a sense of apathy and seem to have lost track of the meaning and greater significance of their lives, you can get them involved in new "quests" or causes to restore the lost meaning, or have a deep, meaningful conversation with them.

General Ways to Help

Most of the time when people are deeply into temperament-related stress, they are unaware of it and can't get themselves out of it without some help. Once people are aware of the impact of not getting their core needs met, they can more easily take responsibility for getting them met on a team (and in life in general) and they can more easily recognize when they are stressed. The rule of thumb when people seem stressed in the ways we have discussed is to see if you can help them get their core needs met. Sometimes just mentioning the stressor can help, especially if they know about their temperament needs. Other times, you have to take some actions to help them.

Use the above information to help your teammates rather than blame them. You may need their help some time too.

WORKING TOGETHER AND MOVING FORWARD 14

We are an interdependent species. Since the beginning of time, people have been working in teams to survive. There was a necessary division of labor among the hunters and gatherers. Families divide up the tasks to be done to take care of the many things that need attention to establish and maintain a residence, keep food on the table, and nurture children. So working together is a given.

At times working together seems like it is more work than it is worth. Yet so much more is possible if we work together well. Teams fill this role in making our work produce more and also be more satisfying. We sincerely hope that you will share the information in this book with your teammates so you can have a common language for looking at what is going on in your team and for discussing your differences.

As you apply the information in this book, we hope you will remember some key points.

- Honor the stages. Yes, sometimes you can skip them, but keep them in your awareness so you can revisit the tasks of each stage when your team gets stuck. Use this book as a reference. Keep it handy.
- Beware of misusing the temperament information to label and blame. Temperament doesn't cause us to do

anything. We still have choices to make. Labeling is often a sign there is more going on that needs to be dealt with. You may need to ask yourself if there is something deeper you would benefit from exploring, either in yourself or in the relationship with the other person.

- Be patient with yourself and your teammates as you all learn about the temperament differences. Playfully, call each other on your stereotypes and biases. Openly share what of the pattern descriptions fit you and what doesn't fit you.
- Find ways to honor the differences. Show your appreciation to your teammates rather than taking their contributions for granted. Practice trying to see things through the lenses of those temperaments you do not easily relate to. Find the things you have in common.

Yes, there is an *I* in Team. You are the *I* in Team and so are your teammates. As you move forward, recognize that we have identified four broad categories of differences and within those differences are more differences. Some people will naturally put more focus on the task aspects of teamwork. Others will naturally put more focus on the process or relationship aspects of teamwork. For many years, experts in the field of understanding individual differences have identified other categorization systems. Some of these relate and work with the temperament model we have presented here. Please visit the Web sites in the references to delve deeper into the subject. At a minimum remember we are all still unique individuals and as individuals we do have influence on teamwork.

We hope you don't settle for being a "do good" team or a "feel good" team and you progress on through the Norming stage and even on to the Performing stage. The rewards are definitely worth the effort, not only in terms of productivity, but in terms of the personal satisfaction you will gain.

APPENDIX

TOOLS

Forming Tool: Map the *I* in the Team [17]

Use this tool to understand the impact temperament may have on your team. Put each team member's name in the appropriate temperament box.

IDEALIST	GUARDIAN
RATIONAL	ARTISAN

How many people does the team have of each temperament?
Artisan ____ Guardian ____ Rational ____ Idealist ____

What's missing from this team?

What are the team strengths?

What are the team blind spots?

What are the potential points of conflict?

Who is in the minority and is likely to get ignored?

How will you address the needs of each team member?

How will you engage the talents on this team?

What will you do to make up for the blind spots on this team?

What is the match of the talents on this team to the nature of the work to be done? If there is a gap, how will you fill it?

If you have remote team members, put asterisks next to their names.

What are the implications of remoteness in this team, based on temperament?

Storming Tool: Team Skills Audit

Use this tool as a positive vehicle to move the team forward together. Understanding what talents and skills are available can help the team utilize people and can also help the team create a development or training plan.

Consider each team member. Fill in each name and temperament. Then write the temperament talents and the person's skills as you see them. Be sure to include your name in this audit.

Don't assume a team member with a certain talent won't have skills in other skill sets. Don't limit your assessment to temperament-related skills.

Team Member	Temperament	Temperament Talents (Diplomacy / Logistics / Strategy / Tactics)	Skills for Doing the Current Work

When the audit is complete, hold a facilitated discussion to share and clarify perceptions and real data about the skills available on your team.

Storming Tool: Map the Team II

Consult your team map on page 172 and answer the following questions:

1. Is there anyone who isn't being heard (because of a minority voice)?

2. What conflict is the team experiencing around
   a. Mismatch of talents and roles (page 95)?
   b. Collision of approaches (page 100)?
   c. Core values (page 105)?
   d. Time orientation (page 106)?
   e. Evaluating solutions (page 107)?
   f. Styles of learning (page 108)?

3. Is the team polarized around any of the following polarities?
   a. Abstract and concrete language
   b. Affiliative and pragmatic roles
   c. Motive and structure interests and focus

4. What are the implications for the team?

5. What can the team do to resolve each conflict?

Storming Tool: Bridging Differences

Sometimes conflicts between individuals impact the whole team. The following tool can help you identify how to deal with those conflicts. Pages 58–59 may help you with the information.

	Mine	His/Hers
Temperament:		
Core Needs:		
Core Values:		
Skill Set:		
	To Me?	To Him/Her?
What's Important?		
	Me?	Him/Her?
Communication Style:		

What aspects of our temperaments do we have in common?

What are our shared interests?

Storming Tool: Shared Interest Worksheet

Use this worksheet to move from the conflicting goals model to the shared goals model on pages 128 and 129.

Our conflicting goals are:

Statements and questions to move from conflicting to shared goals:
- How would the _____ benefit if we worked together?
  (fill in the blank with one of the following)
    - Customer
    - Team
    - Organization
    - Employees
    - (other)

- What do we really want for the _____?
  (fill in the blank with one of the above)

- We agree on _____.
  (fill in the blank with one of the following)
    - High quality
    - Timely delivery
    - A particular quantity
    - Level of involvement
    - (other)

What will work for our situation?

Note: If strong values are violated, you may need to look deeper than temperament patterns to personal values.

NOTES

1. Jon R. Katzenbach and Douglas K. Smith, *The Wisdom of Teams* (New York: HarperCollins, 1993).

2. B.W. Tuckman. "Developmental Sequence in Small Groups," *Psychological Bulletin* 63, no. 6 (1965): 384-99. and J. E. Jones, "Group development: A graphic analysis" in A *Handbook of Structured Experiences for Human Relations Training*, rev ed., ed. J. W. Pfeiffer and J. E. Jones (San Diego, CA: University Associates, 1974), II.

3. R. Beckhard, "Optimizing Team-Building Efforts," *Journal of Contemporary Business* 1 no.3.23–32.

4. The temperament theory presented here is based on Linda Berens understanding and development of the ages old temperament theory. Her unique contributions to this model of understanding human behavior include a focus on core needs, core values, talents, and behaviors as essential aspects of four basic patterns of behavior commonly known as temperament. To maintain continuity, we continue to use the four names developed by David W. Keirsey (Artisan, Guardian, Rational, Idealist) to refer to the four temperament patterns.

5. Adapted from Linda V. Berens and Dario Nardi, *The 16 Personality Types: Descriptions for Self-Discovery* (Huntington Beach, CA: Telos Publications, 1999).

6. Adapted, with permission, from Marci Segal, *Quick Guide to the Four Temperaments and Creativity: A Psychological Understanding of Innovation* (Huntington Beach, CA:Telos Publications, 2003).

7. For more about the foundations of temperament theory, see Ernst Kretschmer, *Physique and Character* (London: Harcourt Brace, 1925) and E. Spränger, *Types of Men.* (1928; rep., New York: Johnson Reprint Company, 1966).

8. David Keirsey and Marilyn Bates, *Please Understand Me.* (Del Mar, Calif.: Prometheus Nemesis Books, 1978).

9. Linda V. Berens, *Understanding Yourself and Others®: An Introduction to Temperament 2.0* (Huntington Beach, CA: Telos Publications, 2000).

10. Adapted from Berens, *Understanding Yourself and Others®: An Introduction to Temperament 2.0* and used, with permission, from Segal, *Quick Guide to the Four Temperaments and Creativity.*

11. Adapted from Berens. *Understanding Yourself and Others®: An Introduction to Temperament 2.0.*

12. Originally formulated by Joseph Luft and Harry Ingham in "The Johari Window: A Graphic Model of Awareness in Interpersonal Relations," in *Group Process: An Introduction to Group Dynamics*, ed. Joseph Luft (Palo Alto, CA: National Press Books, 1963), 10-12.

13. Barry Johnson, *Polarity Management* (Amherst, MA: HRD Press, 1996).

14. Adapted from Dean Tjosvold, *Learning to Manage Conflict.* (New York: Lexington Books, 1993).

15. Adapted from Tjosvold, *Learning to Manage Conflict.*

16. We owe much gratitude to Dr. Sue A. Cooper for identifying the BLM syndrome and thank her for letting us use this valuable acronym in so many places.

17. Adapted from Linda V. Berens, Linda K. Ernst, and Melissa A. Smith, *Quick Guide to the 16 Personality Types and Teams: Applying Team Essentials to Create Effective Teams* (Huntington Beach, CA: Telos Publications, 2004).

INDEX

REFERENCES

Temperament

Berens, Linda V. *Understanding Yourself and Others®: An introduction to temperament 2.0*. Huntington Beach, Calif.: Telos Publications, 2000.

Campbell, Scott. *Quick Guide to the Four Temperaments for Peak Performance: How to Unlock Your Talents to Excel at Work*. Huntington Beach, Calif.: Telos Publications, 2003.

Cooper, Brad. *Quick Guide to the Four Temperaments and Sales: An Introduction to the Groundbreaking Sales® Methods*. Huntington Beach, Calif.: Telos Publications, 2003.

Dossett, Mary, and Julia Mallory. *Results by Design: Survival Skills for Project Managers*. Huntington Beach, Calif.: Telos Publications, 2004.

Dunning, Donna. *Quick Guide to the Four Temperaments and Learning: Practical Tools and Strategies for Enhancing Learning Effectiveness*. Huntington Beach, Calif.: Telos Publications, 2003.

Dunning, Donna. *Quick Guide to the Four Temperaments and Change: Strategies for Navigating Workplace Change*. Huntington Beach, Calif.: Telos Publications, 2004.

Keirsey, David, and Marilyn Bates. *Please Understand Me*. Del Mar, Calif.: Prometheus Nemesis Books, 1978.

Segal, Marci. *Quick Guide to the Four Temperaments and Creativity: A Psychological Understanding of Innovation*. Huntington Beach, Calif.: Telos Publications, 2003.

Specht, David. *Lessons from the Window Seat: Achieving Shared Vision in the Workplace*. Huntington Beach, Calif.: Telos Publications, 2000.

Remote Leadership/Teamwork

Duarte, Deborah L., and Nancy Tennant Snyder. *Mastering Virtual Teams*. San Francisco: Jossey-Bass, Inc., 2001.

Fisher, Kimball, and Mareen Duncan Fisher. *The Distance Manager*. McGraw-Hill, 2001.

Froggatt, Cynthia. *Work Naked*. San Francisco: Jossey-Bass, Inc., 2001.

Gerke, Susan K., and Linda V. Berens. *Quick Guide to Interaction Styles and Working Remotely: Strategies for Leading and Working in Virtual Teams*. Huntington Beach, Calif.: Telos Publications, 2003.

Hoefling, Trina. *Working Virtually*. Virginia: Stylus Publishing, LLC, 2001.

Kostner, Jaclyn. *Virtual Leadership*. New York: Warner Books, 1994.

Odenwald, Sylvia B. *Global Solutions for Teams*. Chicago: Irwin Professional Publishing, 1996.

O'Hara-Deveraux, Mary and Robert Johansen. *Global Work: Bridging Distance, Culture, and Time*. San Francisco: Jossey-Bass, Inc., 1994.

Teams and Related Topics

Berens, Linda V., Linda K. Ernst, and Melissa A. Smith. *Quick Guide to the 16 Personality Types and Teams: Applying Team Essentials to Create Effective Teams*. Huntington Beach, Calif.: Telos Publications, 2004.

Johnson, Barry. *Polarity Management*. Amherst, MA: HRD Press, 1996.

Kaner, Sam. *Facilitator's Guide to Participatory Decision-Making*. Canada: New Society Publoishers, 1996.

Katzenbach, Jon R., and Douglas K. Smith. *The Wisdom of Teams*. New York: HarperCollins, 1999.

Nash, Susan. *Turning Team Performance Inside Out*. Palo Alto, Calif.: Davies-Black Publishing, 2000.

Nash, Susan., and Courtney Bolin. *Teamwork from the Inside Out Fieldbook*. Palo Alto, Calif.: Davies-Black Publishing, 2003.

On the Internet

4temperaments.com: www.4temperaments.com

16types.com®: www.16types.com

BestFitType.com: www.bestfittype.com

Susan Gerke: www.susangerke.com

Telos Publications: www.telospublications.com

TRI (Linda V. Berens): www.tri-network.com

ABOUT THE
AUTHORS

 Susan Gerke is the president of Gerke Consulting & Development and "helps people work better, together." Susan has been in business since 1998 following twenty-one years working for IBM. She was a manager for IBM as well as a technical support representative and a management and leadership development professional.

Susan's focus since 1989 has been in designing, customizing, and implementing leadership and teamwork programs, meeting the needs of executives, managers, and employees in a wide number of companies and industries. She has applied her skill and knowledge in facilitation, consulting, curriculum development, and coaching. Susan has developed and delivered experiential programs in a number of areas, including remote work, managing conflict, teams and teamwork, leadership, mentoring, and facilitation skills.

Susan is a specialist in instruments and is certified for SYMLOG, Herrmann Brain Dominance® (HBDI), Element B, the Myers-Briggs Type Indicator® (MBTI®), and the Management Team Roles Indicator™ (MTR-i®). She is on the faculty of TRI and is InterStrength™ certified.

Susan has a bachelor's degree in statistics from California Polytechnic State University, San Luis Obispo. She is a graduate of the University Associates Human Resources and Organizational Development Intern program.

Linda V. Berens is the founder and Director of TRI (formerly Temperament Research Institute), a corporate consulting and training organization. TRI is one of eight organizations in the United States that qualifies professionals to administer the Myers-Briggs Type Indicator® instrument. TRI also certifies professionals in the Interstrength™ assessments and method, the Ideal Team Profile Questionnaire™ (ITPQ™) and the Management Team Role-indicator® (MTR-i®).

Linda holds a doctorate in psychology and serves as an adjunct faculty member in the Masters in Organizational Leadership program at Chapman University. She is the author of *Understanding Yourself and Others®: An Introduction to Temperament; Understanding Yourself and Others®: An Introduction to Interaction Styles;* and *Dynamics of Personality Type: Understanding and Applying Jung's Cognitive Processes* and the coauthor of *The 16 Personality Types: Descriptions for Self-Discovery; Understanding Yourself and Others®: An Introduction to the Personality Type Code; Quick Guide to the 16 Personality Types and Teams; Groundbreaking Sales® Skills; Working Together: A Personality-Centered Approach to Management* and other books and training materials.

Linda is an organizational consultant and has spent over thirty years training professionals in the field as well as helping individuals and teams recognize their strengths, transcend their weaknesses, and work together better.

Both Linda and Susan are available to work with your organization on the subject of teams and temperament. Linda specializes in whole-organization implementation as well as individual and team development. Susan specializes in helping organizations, teams, and individuals with remote work, leadership, and team development.

They can be reached at
Susan K. Gerke: www.susangerke.com
Linda V. Berens: www.tri-network.com, 1-800-700-4874